EX LIBRIS

SCOTTISH CLANS

A very peculiar history™

Càirdeas is comain is eòlas

Kinship and community and friendship

Traditional Gaelic saying

For my kith and kin

FMacD

Editor: Stephen Haynes

Published in Great Britain in MMXIII by
Book House, an imprint of
The Salariya Book Company Ltd
25 Marlborough Place, Brighton BN1 1UB
www.salariya.com
www.book-house.co.uk

HB ISBN-13: 978-1-908759-90-0

1 3 5 7 9 8 6 4 2

A CIP catalogue record for this book is available
from the British Library.

Printed and bound in India.

Printed on paper from sustainable sources.

Visit our **new** online shop at
shop.salariya.com
for great offers, gift ideas, all our new releases
and free postage and packaging.

SCOTTISH
CLANS

A very peculiar history™

Fiona Macdonald

Created and designed by
David Salariya

"

Cuimhnich có leis
a tha thu.

Remember those from whom you came.

Traditional Gaelic saying

Contents

"

Does your blood run thick
with the stories of your gallant
Scottish ancestors – tales of
kilted warriors fighting
the march of time amid the
heather-clad hills of
the Highlands?

Vacation Scotland website

"

INTRODUCTION

Scotland! Oh, the misty mountains, lonely lochs, grassy glens. It's rugged, rainy and romantic. Once the home of hardy heroes, craggy castles, canny crofters – not to mention fine minds, great industries and world-changing inventions. Now busy renewing itself, through oil, green energy, creative businesses and a celebration of Scottish culture – including Scotland's dramatic and enthralling history. Its largest industries delight the pleasure-seeking and the pleasure-loving: tourism, whisky and golf.

A happy thought!

Family matters

Scotland is also famous – of course – as the home of the clans. All round the world, people of Scottish heritage proudly claim their own clan membership, name, tartan, ancestral homeland, and much, much more. To them and to many others, the very mention of the word 'clan' inspires dramatic, even cinematic, images – to say nothing of whole libraries full of historical fiction, featuring characters such as 'a massive Gael swathed in plaid and hostility' or 'a bewitching lass whose flaming red hair matches the fire of her spirit'. It all adds up to a strong and deeply reassuring sense of nostalgia.

What's in a name? If the name happens to be affiliated to a Scottish clan, the answer is an unparalleled connection to history, geography, literature and romance….Those lucky enough to be linked with a clan have access to a rich and ready-made history and an instant kinship which stretches around the globe.

Gillian Bowditch in *The Scotsman*,
27 November 2004

I am a Scot…

In 2009, the Year of the Homecoming, advertisements like this, suitably adapted for each target audience, reached almost 95 million friends of Scotland, all round the world.

I am a Scot.
I buy the first round.
I'm true to my word.
I've bagged a munro.
I never miss the 19th hole.
I've taken the High Road and the Low Road.
I don't know the words to 'Auld Lang Syne'.
But I know what they mean.

I'm a New Yorker, but I'm a Scot at heart…

EventScotland, 2010

a munro: a Scottish mountain over 3,000 ft (914.4 m) high. To 'bag' one is to climb it.

A world of Scots

By the late 20th century there were probably ten times more people of Scottish descent living overseas than residing in Scotland. That's between 50 and 60 million worldwide. If they, their Granny, or their cousin's great-auntie Nellie had a Scottish clan surname, then Scotland was also their country. Like Scots in Scotland, they might sometimes mock romantic movies and novels – but the thoughts and feelings conjured up by images of clans, kilts and misty mountains showed that they belonged.

And that, dear readers, is what clans are all about. They are real and they're important. To be a member of a clan means to belong – to a people, a family, the land – now, then, for ever:

> Or if on life's uncertain main
>> Mishap shall mar thy sail;
> If faithful, wise, and brave in vain,
> Woe, want, and exile thou sustain
>> Beneath the fickle gale;

Waste not a sigh on fortune changed,
On thankless courts, or friends estranged,
But come where kindred worth shall smile,
To greet thee in the lonely isle.

Sir Walter Scott, *The Lady of the Lake*
(Canto Second), 1810

This book will look at the history of Scottish clans: who they were, where they lived, how they fought and feasted, and how they struggled to survive in some of the least hospitable territory in Europe. We will see how clans faced attack: from ambitious kings, profiteering farmers, and changing economic conditions that brought a new commercial and industrial lifestyle to North Britain. Of course, clans were also in danger from each other; and, in fierce family quarrels and rivalries, sometimes even from themselves.

We will also see how, once old ways of clan life had safely disappeared for ever, clans became the focus of intense, romantic – and sometimes inaccurate – interest, all round the world. It's a very peculiar story…

Brigadoon to Braveheart

If ye love someone deeply, anythin' is possible.

From the original 1947 stage musical *Brigadoon*

Yes, anything's possible – even a magical village in the Scottish Lowlands, full of tartan-clad clansfolk wearing fantasy Highland dress. Frozen in time to preserve its perfection, the wee fairytale hamlet of Brigadoon appeared and disappeared in front of a pair of American innocents abroad as they roamed through studio stages swathed in Celtic mists and scattered with the bonnie purple heather.

From 1954's *Brigadoon* to 1995's *Braveheart*, Hollywood has certainly shown its love for Scotland, and incidentally performed an invaluable service for the Scottish tourist and heritage industries. But there is more, much more, behind the success of these Scottish-themed cinema epics.

Certainly, glamorous superstars (Gene Kelly, Cyd Charisse, Mel Gibson) are an attraction. So are the splendid action sequences: mock Scottish dancing and mock battles between knights and clansmen. There's nostalgia aplenty, and heroism, and romance – and, in *Braveheart*, magnificent Scottish scenery. (Plans to film *Brigadoon* in Scotland were ruined by rain.)

But both films also celebrate traditional clan values – steadfast determination, passionate love, loyalty, courage, honour – that would make any country feel proud of itself, and stir the hearts of millions of Scots and Scots-lovers worldwide.

What do we know?

Clan history is rich in incident, myth and legend. Scholars have spilled an enormous amount of ink debating precisely what happened in Scotland's past. Sometimes it's hard to know how to sort out fact from fantasy, or keep up to date with the latest historical findings. And so, before we begin, here is a very brief outline sketch of how Scottish clans rose, and fell – and have been reinvented:

c.AD 60 Roman historians speak of Celtic tribes, with leaders, living in Scotland. But tribes and clans are not the same. Clans are linked by a shared belief (whether true or false) in kinship; tribes may not be.

c.650 People in western Scotland live in kin-groups, and trace their descent from ancient, mostly mythological, heroes. They pay tribute (taxes in goods) to their leaders.

c.1100 Some of the first evidence of groups called clans emerges, from northeast Scotland. Clans have leaders, who own land and collect tribute from people living there.

c.1150 Scottish king David I brings Anglo-Norman knights to Scotland. He declares that all land belongs to the king. He gives land (with people living on it) to the knights in return for rent and duties. The knights become the leaders of new clans.

c.1164 Death of Somerled (Gaelic *Somhairle* – pronounced 'Sorley'), a part-Viking, part-Gaelic warlord who ruled a kingdom in the far west of

Scotland. He was the founder of the largest Scottish clan, the MacDonalds. Other powerful men throughout Scotland also found clans at around this time.

1263 Norwegian rulers lose control of the northwest Highlands and Islands. The MacDonald Lords of the Isles rule an independent kingdom there until 1493.

c.1300–1500 More new clans develop, as sons of existing clan chiefs break away, conquer new land, produce descendants and attract followers. People living on clan lands may take the name of the clan chief, without being related to him. Some rich, grand, noble clan leaders no longer live on clan lands.

c.1300–1513 Rival clan leaders quarrel and fight; some support rival claimants to the Scottish crown. Some chiefs have private armies of *gallowglasses* (trained mercenaries); many clansmen serve as mercenaries overseas. Clansmen skirmish and raid cattle. Border *reivers* (raiders) take cattle and fight each other. Kings, chiefs, clansmen all unite to fight off English invaders.

SCOTTISH CLANS

c.1300–1700 Kings try to subdue the power of clans in the Highlands and Islands, and also in Galloway and the Borders. Loyal clan leaders, especially the Campbells and Gordons, are rewarded with land and influence.

c.1493–1625 Collapse of the 'kingdom' of the Lords of the Isles. Start of the 'Age of the Forays': a time of feuds and fighting, hatred and revenge between smaller, lawless clans, especially in the west (Lochaber, Wester Ross and Argyll) and the islands of the Hebrides.

c.1600–1750 Many clansmen and women emigrate. Like other Scottish landowners, clan chiefs start to take a commercial interest in their estates (cattle, timber, iron, then sheep). The bond between chiefs and clansmen weakens. Clansmen and women suffer hardship.

Meanwhile, clan leaders take opposing sides in national political crises: Union of the Crowns, Civil War, Act of Union, Jacobite Rebellion.

1747–1782 Jacobites defeated. Government bans Highland clothes, music etc. Poor clansmen seek work in British armies. Start of Highland Clearances in the Great Glen.

c.1800–1900 Romantic, nostalgic interest in a fantasy version of Highland Scotland, featuring clans and tartans. Queen Victoria's love for Balmoral. Scotland's 'wilderness' becomes a playground for rich tourists who enjoy huntin', shootin', fishin'.

During this same period, Highland Clearances are at their worst: clansmen and women are forced off their lands. Many emigrate; others find work in Lowland cities. Old clan townships disappear; crofting system develops.

c.1900–1960 Scholarly interest in clans and Highland culture: Gaelic language, music, dance, poetry, clothes, architecture, archaeology, traditional sports. Crofting continues.

c.1960–present Revival of living Gaelic culture and way of life in Scotland, encouraged by governments. Growth of cultural tourism and heritage industries. Tartan becomes fashionable. Clan societies flourish in many parts of the world.

"

Is treasa tuath na Tighearna.

The tribe is stronger than the chief.

Gaelic proverb

"

CHAPTER ONE

WHAT IS A CLAN?

I n 1411, Donald, Lord of the Isles, gave a rousing speech to his clansmen, assembled and ready to fight at Harlaw near Inverurie in Aberdeenshire. He urged them:

Sons of Colla, be brave in danger...

Alas, by the end of the day almost 1,000 of Donald's soldiers were not alive to remember his bold words. But his speech was revealing. He – and perhaps his loyal clan followers – liked to think that they were all descended from the same great royal hero, Colla, High King of Ireland, who had lived long, long ago. They were literally brothers in arms.

At its very simplest, the word *clan* means 'children'. The modern English word comes from the Scottish Gaelic *clann*. That was first recorded in writing shortly before AD 1400 – not in English, but in the Scots language used at that time by Scottish kings and parliaments. However, its origins are much older; similar words for offspring are found in Celtic languages that have been spoken in the British Isles for over 2,000 years: Irish *cland*, Welsh *plant*. *Clann* is also related to the Latin word *planta*, which can mean 'offshoot' as well as 'plant growing in the ground'.

The ties that bind

Family and heredity were obviously very important to early Scottish people. Why else would they have had several different words to describe them, all with precise shades of meaning? As well as naming their clan, Gaelic-speaking Scots referred to their kindred (*cineal*; say 'ke-nel'), their seed or progeny (*sìol*; 'shee-ul') and their descendants (*sliochd*; 'sleechg'). All these words describe close, intimate, biological relationships – ties of blood.

From the very earliest times, the humblest Scottish people were aware of precisely who they, and their relatives, were. Traditionally, men and women in the Highlands could recite a list of their ancestors' names going back maybe ten generations. The blood tie mattered most to clan chiefs and their close relatives, who passed rank, title and land from one generation to the next. For them, the word *clann* signified (and still signifies) their actual biological family.

However, much more often, belonging to a clan meant feeling bound together by ties of lordship, loyalty, geography, neighbourliness, a shared name and a shared struggle to stay alive. Clansmen and women may also, when it suited them, have shared a willingness to claim kinship with a real or mythological ancestor, lost in the mists of time.

Ancient myths, modern science

The Clan Donald (modern surnames MacDonald, MacDonell and many, many more) is the largest Scottish clan, with members living all round the world. Traditionally, the whole clan claimed descent from two great heroes: Somerled (see page 14), a seafaring warrior who died around 1164, and warlord High King Colla Uais who ruled in Ireland around AD 300. These traditions were preserved for centuries by *seanchaidhean* (clan historians, or bards; say 'shen-ech-ih-een'). They encouraged and entertained (even if they did not always convince) the millions of men, women and children who listened to them.

In the early 21st century, scientists using modern genetic analysis techniques decided to see whether DNA testing would support the traditional version of MacDonald history. Their findings were revealing in two – no, three – ways:

1. Test results suggest that Somerled was a Viking! (After all, the name is Norse; it means 'summer raider'.) A Scottish Viking, true: but his

ancestors seem to have been at least half Norwegian, and, in 11th-century Scotland, 'Norwegian' meant 'pirate'. Looking at the non-Viking side of his family, DNA testers suggest that Somerled's distant ancestors may just perhaps be connected to Irish High King Colla.

2. DNA evidence also suggests that today's chiefs of several branches of Clan Donald are related to each other. Their DNA is untypical among Highland men in Scotland, but much more common in Norway. They may well be descended from Somerled.

So the traditional histories seem to be pretty accurate, then? Yes – and no:

3. DNA evidence from ordinary male members of the MacDonald clan today shows a different genetic pattern to that of their leaders. Only one in five ordinary MacDonald men may be descended from Norwegians (maybe even Somerled himself); a similar proportion may – like Somerled – have ancestors among the Irish warlords, warriors, traders, slaves and sailors who crossed and recrossed the Irish Sea during the past 2,500 years.

However, over half the male MacDonalds tested so far are descended from men who have lived in Scotland since the end of the last Ice Age. In Scotland, that was between 10,000 and 8,000 years ago. How do we know? These 'majority Macdonalds' (if we may call them that) are members of genetic subgroups typically found in the Highlands, and in other parts of far-north and far-west Europe. They are members of the MacDonald clan, but they are not descended from Coll or Somerled, or related to MacDonald clan leaders.

Want to find out more? See:
http://www.scotsman.com/news/arts/using_science_to_trace_your_scottish_roots_1_465447
and
http://dna-project.clan-donald-usa.org/

Who we are

If we believe the scientific evidence, clan membership was clearly not always biological. As the famous old Scottish proverb declared:

All Stewarts are not sib [brother] to the king.

In fact, DNA research suggests that around 25 per cent of males with the surname Stewart are related to Scottish kings James IV and James V, of the Stewart ruling dynasty. However, just like family blood ties, clan relationships were tremendously important. They gave Scottish people a sense of identity. Clan members took pride in a famous clan name, a dramatic clan history, and the brave deeds of clan heroes.

Belonging to a clan also created a sense of brotherhood among members. It established a natural, unquestionable bond between them; what in the world could be stronger? It encouraged loyalty, to clan brothers and to clan leaders. It promoted mutual support, help, charity. In past times, when Scottish law and order was often maintained at sword-point and there was no welfare state to care for the weak or helpless, men, women and children relied on their families, and their clans, to survive.

> There is no earthly thing I put in balance with my kindred… my guard, my glory and my honour.

Lord Lovat, leader of Clan Fraser, c.1745

put in balance with: give equal importance to; guard: protectors and protected.

Fine words, MacShimi! (That's Gaelic for 'Son of Simon', the traditional form of address for leaders of Clan Fraser.) The leader of a clan might not be related by blood to the poorest cottagers sharing his surname. But, if a good and responsible man, he could still be a 'father' to them.

Brothers *and* sisters?

But how did women relate to these bands of clan brothers? How did clan membership shape their identity? Until marriage, a Scottish woman belonged to her father's clan. After the wedding, she was expected to be loyal to her husband's family – although this did not always happen. Traditionally a woman did not change her name on marriage. However, her children took her husband's name and reckoned their lineage following the male line.

Until around 1600 it was not uncommon for clan chiefs to have more than one wife: one formally recognised by the Christian church, and others 'married' according to Gaelic tradition. Typically, a man and a woman lived together for a year and a day. After that they might part amicably, with no dishonour, or stay together for longer, especially if a baby was on the way. So long as ancient custom was obeyed, all the children would be legitimate (although, from around AD 1000, the Church began to disagree with this). A large family of many sons was a source of pride, and clear proof of the chief's virility (one chief of Clan Urquhart boasted of having fathered 25 sons). But it also often led to quarrels over land and inheritance, since – except among Anglo-Norman newcomers to Scotland (see page 53) – a chief's eldest son did not automatically inherit his father's land.

In all but the poorest families, a bride brought a *tocher* (dowry) with her; originally it was paid in cattle. Some clan chiefs, such as the Campbells, were famous for increasing their family's wealth and influence by choosing brides with plenty of money or land, or excellent political connections. Other clans tried to keep property within the family.

Is fearr bean ghlic na crann is fearann.

Better a wise wife than plough and land.

Gaelic proverb

Lonely lady

The last male chief of the MacRuari clan was assassinated – in a nunnery (don't ask) – in 1346. His only heir was a sister, Amie of Garmoran. She was a rich prize in the marriage stakes; whoever wed her would eventually take control of all her father's land in the far west of mainland Scotland. Amie's hand was hotly contested; it was won by a distant cousin, John of Islay. Like Amie, he was a descendant of Somerled – and in 1337 he became the first chief to style himself 'Lord of the Isles'.

Poor Amie! Although she was a loyal wife to John and produced three sons for him, he seems to have made plans to leave her as soon as her father died. The couple were finally divorced in 1350. John married again, even more ambitiously; his new wife was the daughter of King David II's chosen heir, Robert Stewart, High Steward of Scotland. According to law, John should have lost control of the MacRuari lands when he left Amie, but King David granted him a charter confirming his right to keep them. It would be many years before Amie's son Ranald won them back again.

Amie lived alone, apart from servants, for the rest of her life. She gave money to build or rebuild churches, and to enlarge her family's castles. One, Castle Tioram (Dry Castle; pronounced 'Chirrum') in Moidart, still survives in ruins. In spite of its unhappy past, it is one of the most romantic places in the world.

Amie also took revenge on her ex-husband, in her own not-so-sweet way. She caused a deadly quarrel between him and the friend who had first advised him to seek a divorce. Amie told John of Islay that his friend had complained, in public, that he'd been given lodgings in John's castle that 'stank like a dog-kennel'. This was a very grave insult. Not only were dogs and their excrement deeply unhygienic and ritually unclean; for a clan chief to be a bad or careless host was unforgivable.

Since brides usually came from families that were friendly to their husbands' clans, or shared political opinions with them, conflicts of interest were uncommon. But they did happen. For example, in 1745, Isabel Haldane had a famous quarrel with her husband, clan chieftain Charles Stewart of Appin. She was a keen Jacobite (see page 151); he was unwilling to lead his clansmen into what he feared would be a dangerous, futile rebellion.

Isabel was exasperated. She is said to have exclaimed:

If you are not willing to be commander of the Appin men, stay at home and take care of the house, and I will go and command them myself.

Quoted in Maggie Craig, *Damn' Rebel Bitches: The Women of the '45*, 1997, p. 20

> Every Highlander can talk
> of his ancestors…

Dr Samuel Johnson, *A Journey to the
Western Islands of Scotland*, 1775

CHAPTER TWO

WARLORDS, FAIRIES AND MONSTERS

T horfinn the Mighty (died c.1065) was not a man to fall foul of, especially if you were alone and unarmed. He is described in the *Orkneyinga Saga* (a prose epic written in Iceland around 1230) as:

> exceptionally tall and strong, ugly and hard-featured, with lots of black hair, a big nose and bushy eyebrows…aggressive…eager for fame and fortune. He won battles because he made clever plans; he was also very brave.

The saga adds that, at the height of his power, Thorfinn controlled Orkney and Shetland, together with the Hebrides, Caithness and

Sutherland, and a large part of northern Scotland – and that he conquered seven Scottish 'kingdoms'.

That last claim is probably an exaggeration, but Thorfinn and raiders like him – from Scandinavia, Ireland, south of the Border in England, and directly across the North Sea – attacked and captured vast areas of Scottish land between around AD 400 and 1100. Because of them, Scotland was divided for centuries into several separate, rival, power-blocs. It was most definitely not a united nation.

Mighty men like Thorfinn and Somerled (whom we first met on page 14) were warlords. They had armies, which they kept loyal by gifts of land and treasure; they had servants, noble and humble; some had priests; they had close – and sometimes dangerous – kindred. They schemed and plotted and fought and killed, fired by ambition. These men were leaders – to their families, their kinsfolk, their soldiers. They fought hard and they thought big. And most of them aimed to rule as much of Scotland as possible.

It would be many centuries before a single man, however bold, however strong, however brave a fighter, could achieve that royal ambition. And, while rival warlords and early Scottish kings struggled to keep control of the lands they had conquered, clans and clan chiefs grew strong, and filled the power vacuum.

Where did clans come from?

Who lived in Scotland while kings and warlords were fighting for power? Did Scottish people already belong to clans before the time of Thorfinn, Somerled or Kenneth MacAlpin? If not, where did clans come from?

All kinds of fanciful theories have been put forward about early Scottish society. Most are loosely based on information from Ireland rather than Scotland, and especially from a collection known today as the 'Brehon Laws'. (*Brehon* is Irish Gaelic for 'judge'.) These claim to be a record of social customs and criminal penalties in Ireland, dating from the time of St Patrick (around AD 500) or even earlier.

In fact, scholars think that the Brehon Laws were first written down by Christian priests in Ireland some time between AD 600 and 700. Probably, the priests based their writings on old traditions, or on the social customs that they saw around them. Very probably, they also adjusted the old laws to fit in with their own Christian ideas of good behaviour. In either case, the Brehon Laws can give us some information about western Scotland, which had close links with people living on the opposite side of the Irish Sea – but only if they are read with care and caution.

The Brehon Laws list three different kinds of kinship. The closest ties are between people descended from one grandfather (*gelfine*). The next closest share a great-grandfather (*derbfine*). The most loosely linked are descended from a great-great-grandfather (*indfine*). But, however close or distant the link, the laws assume that everyone will belong to one kin group or another. Without kin, a man or woman was a stranger, an outsider, alone and without protection. Without even a name.

Were things the same in Scotland? In some ways, yes – so far as we can tell. Around AD 650, an unknown ruler gave orders to count all the households in Dál Riata (a kingdom in southwest Scotland) and list what they owed in tribute (tax paid in goods); it is the oldest census to survive in the British Isles. Its findings are preserved in a later text, the *Senchus fer nAlban* (History of the Men of Scotland), compiled around 950. Here is an extract:

> Cenél Loairnd [the kin or descendants of Lorne] has 430 houses; [it must provide] two seven-bench ships [for] every 20 houses, [ready to sail] in a sea expedition.

In the census, the people of Dál Riata are divided into three separate groups. Each group is said to comprise the *cenél* (descendants) of a long-dead ancestor – a hero. The Cenél nGabráin lived in Kintyre, the Cenél Loairnd had their homes in Argyll, and the Cenél nÓengusa occupied the islands of Islay and Jura.

Dead – but not forgotten

True or false, claims of descent from long-dead heroes gave rise to some splendid stories:

• **Clan Campbell** boasted of their kinship with mythical Irish warrior Diarmuid Ua Duibhne (say 'Dermot O'Dyna'). He fought with enchanted weapons, inflicting wounds that never healed, and was so magically handsome that no woman could stop herself falling in love with him. Gored to death by a monster wild boar, Diarmuid was brought back to life by the Celtic god of love.

The Campbells also honoured a heroic forefather, Cailean Mór (Great Colin; say 'Calan More'), who died in battle in 1294.

• The ancestor of **Clan MacNeill** – many of whose members still live on the island of Barra in the Hebrides – is said to have been a warrior-prince who settled there in the 11th century. He, in turn, claimed descent from legendary Irish ruler Niall of the Nine Hostages, who became king of Ireland after braving a deep, dark forest and daring to kiss the 'loathly lady' – a horrendous hag who (of course!) then turned into a beautiful maiden.

• **Clan Murray** claimed descent from the family of the murderous MacBheatha mac Fhionnlaigh (say 'Mac Be-ah mac Finlay') – Shakespeare's Macbeth. But Shakespeare's story, however thrilling, is full of historical errors. The real Macbeth was royal deputy in the vast north-Scottish territory of Moray; he became king of Scotland c.1040–1057.

• **Clan Matheson**'s Gaelic name translates as 'Son of the Bear'. Perhaps disappointingly, historians suggest that this simply means 'child of a Viking named Bjorn or Bjarni'.

• However, we soon find enchantment again in the pedigree of **Clan MacLeod**. Descended from Olaf, King of the Isle of Man, the fourth MacLeod chief was reputed to have married a beautiful fairy. The magic flag she gave him – it brings both victory and doom – still hangs in Dunvegan Castle on the Isle of Skye.

• Most ambitious of all, **Clan Urquhart** traced its ancestry right back to Adam.

Land and leaders

Shared ancestry provided a way of distinguishing between one group and another; between 'them' and 'us'. But later clans were bound together by more than that. They had leaders, and they had land.

The Brehon Laws list inheritance rules that are clearly designed to keep land within a kin-group, and to give all group members rights over kin land. Did this happen in early Scotland also? Maybe. But it's clear that powerful men in Scotland also had rights to own and give away land. The story opposite is told in Gaelic notes added around 1130 to a manuscript called 'The Book of Deer', belonging to a monastery in northeast Scotland.

Bede the Pict was *mormaer* (king's deputy or chief officer; say 'mor mer' or 'mor vair') in the district of Buchan. Other donors mentioned in the Book of Deer include Comgell son of Cainnech, '*taoiseach* (chief or leader; say 'tea-sosch') of Clann Channan'. This is a vital clue – and one of the earliest factual written references to a Scottish clan.

A tale of St Columba

St Columba (died AD 597) and Drostan, his disciple, were far from their home on the island of Iona. They met Bede the Pict; he gave them his monastery at Aberlour. Saint and disciple then moved on to another monastic community; it pleased Columba very much, 'for it was full of the grace of God'. Columba asked Bede to give him that monastery, as well, but Bede refused.

Soon afterwards, Bede's son fell dangerously ill. He begged the saint to cure the boy, but Columba was unwilling. So Bede gave him a generous gift of land, including the second monastery. St Columba and Drostan 'made a prayer' and Bede's son recovered.

Source: http://www.ucc.ie/celt/published/G102007/

How can we bridge the gap between the kin-groups mentioned in the census of Dál Raita, around 650, and the reference to a clan and clan chief in the Book of Deer almost 500 years later? Using what we know of

Somerled's life, and genetics, and the Book of Deer, here is one possible scenario:

Kin-groups lived in Scotland; very probably they had leaders, who may originally have been their own kin. Strong men like Thorfinn and Somerled arrived from elsewhere and seized land; home-grown warlords like Macbeth (mormaer of Moray, and the hero or villain of Shakespeare's play) fought to win land, too. The winners demanded tribute and loyalty from families living on the land they had conquered. The weaker kin-group leaders died fighting invaders, or sought protection from stronger warlords. The warlords' sons followed their fathers as leaders, or else broke away and set up new clans of their own. They may have had no blood-ties to the kin-groups whose taxes they collected and whose land and lives they controlled. One thing seems certain: however they began, by around 1130 clans were alive and well, and living in Scotland.

'Another for Hector!'

The ancient custom of fostering also strengthened links between chiefs and the men and women who followed them. From babyhood, chiefs' sons were handed over to trusted and respected clan families to be brought up and educated. Seven years was the traditional length of time spent away from home. For the fostering family, receiving a child was an honour as well as a duty; they were also well paid, usually with cattle. In return, chiefs' families fostered the children of senior clansmen and friendly clan leaders.

A Scottish proverb shows how strong the ties between a fostered son and the children of his foster family might be: 'Affectionate is a man to his friend, but a foster-brother is as the life-blood of his heart.'

In 1561, at the Battle of Inverkeithing, seven foster-brothers of chief Hector MacLean of Duart stepped up to defend him, one after the other, each with the cry 'Another for Hector'. They were all killed – and so, at last, was he.

66

The whole barbarity of that nation was softened…as if forgetting their natural fierceness they submitted their necks to the laws which the royal gentleness dictated.

Royal courtier Aelred of Rievaulx, praising King David I's government of Scotland, c.1153

99

CHAPTER THREE

ROYALTY – AND LOYAL LORDS

King David I of Scotland (ruled 1124–1153) was an unlikely revolutionary. The son of a saint (St Margaret, canonised in 1250), he was imprisoned by his uncle, exiled from his homeland aged 9, befriended by a great English king (Henry I, who became his brother-in-law), and was showered with land, riches and noble titles after marrying a great heiress.

After years in England, fighting as a knight, David returned to Scotland around 1124. He had 'rubbed off all tarnish of Scottish barbarity through being polished by…

friendship with us', as English chronicler Henry of Huntingdon rather tactlessly put it – and he brought with him many new ideas.

The Scotland that David found had been ruled by kings for over 200 years. But it was hardly settled; rival kings and warlords were still keen to take over Scottish territory.

Neither Orkney and Shetland, nor the Hebrides, nor Ross, Caithness and Sutherland in the far north, Argyll in the west, nor Galloway in the south were under Scottish crown control.

David spent years fighting to win lands south of the Forth estuary from the English, and the great territory of Moray, in the northeast, from rival branches of his own kin.

King meets clans

If we could travel back in time, to join King David I as he made his way through Scotland (or, at least, the parts of it that he controlled), what would we see? What would Scotland be like?

• We would find an intensely rural country: scattered villages, no towns, no roads, no coins. Most people spoke Gaelic, except in the far north (where they spoke Norse, the language of the Vikings), and in the far southeast and the disputed Borderlands, where a new language – Scots – was slowly developing. David and his close associates spoke French, and some Gaelic, too.

• In Lowland and Highland areas, we would see ordinary Scottish men, women and children – farmers, fisherfolk, sailors. Compared with today, their lives were poor and tough and short. But they survived, by being remarkably self-sufficient, and by relying on help from their friends – and their kin.

• We would also meet King David's mightiest subjects: warlords who had decided that it might, for the moment, be to their advantage to be on the same side as the king. Some were junior members of the royal family; others held royal government posts, such as mormaer (see page 40). Their duty was to defend the Scottish king's lands, and maintain good order within them. Such men were essential, but also very dangerous. They had local knowledge and long-established political networks. What if they quarrelled with the king, or rebelled against him?

• Below the rank of royal prince or mormaer, but more numerous, were the *taoisichean*, the 'first men', or clan chiefs. (A prince or a mormaer might also be chief of a clan.) Each chief claimed an area of land as his clan's *dùthchas* (rightful, ancestral homeland, place of belonging; say 'doochus') and protected the people who lived there. But few chiefs welcomed, or even acknowledged, royal control.

• Clans fought each other as well as invaders. Clan chiefs could call on armies of sons, brothers, nephews and ordinary clansmen;

they might be helped sometimes by fighters from friendly clans and perhaps by mercenary soldiers (see page 50).

Might is right?

The early clan chiefs held their clan lands 'by right of the sword': they won them and kept them by fighting. They acknowledged no overlord, except God. If clans were defeated in battle, then the right to own and exploit their land passed to their victorious enemies. To an ambitious king like David I, who aimed to control all of Scotland, these free, independent, warring clans were an obvious threat to law and order – and to the peaceful enjoyment of his time on the throne. But how could he control them?

David decided to import what was – for Scotland – a revolutionary new idea. It was copied from what he had seen and learned at the English royal court, but was also fashionable among rulers in many other parts of Europe. For royal people in power, it had many attractions.

Gallowglasses

From around 1200 until 1600, troops of well-trained, well-armed mercenary soldiers sailed from Scotland to fight in foreign wars. Most went to Ireland; their name – *gallóglach* – is Irish Gaelic for 'foreign young soldier'. Others fought in Scandinavia and France.

Gallowglasses were mostly recruited from northwest Scotland, an area with many Viking traditions. They were elite troops, who served in companies of around 100 men led by an experienced commander. They fought on foot, and were typically deployed in defensive positions. They wore coats of chainmail and cone-shaped iron helmets; their favoured weapons were two-handed battleaxes, claymores (long swords) and spears. Each soldier might be accompanied by one or two young grooms.

After fighting in Ireland, many Scottish mercenaries settled there. Modern surnames with gallowglass connections include McCabe, McDonnell, McRory, Sheehy and Sweeney.

David claimed that, as king, all the land of Scotland belonged to him, and that he was the overlord of every man, woman and child living there. If existing major landowners (whoever they were: warlords, mormaers, clan chiefs) swore allegiance to him, and agreed to 'pay' for their land by fighting for the king when he summoned them, then they could continue to occupy it. But from now on they would be tenants, not absolute owners. If they did not accept David's new idea, then he would take the land away from them, by force if necessary.

David was just one man — although formidable, and with his own army. How could he impose this new idea on a whole nation? He decided to import eager, ambitious knights from south of the Border, and give them land. The new knights' future rank and wealth — and the safety of their descendants — would be firmly linked to the wellbeing and stability of David's Scottish kingdom. They were bound to be loyal, at least in the beginning. In their turn, the new landholders would lease portions of their new estates to the ordinary families who lived there, in return for 'gifts' of food and labour-service in fields and farms, and an obligation to fight in their landlord's army.

A new way to rule

To further strengthen his hold on power, and promote peaceful, profitable trade, David introduced many more changes to the way Scotland was governed. He built strong royal castles (the oldest surviving parts of Edinburgh Castle date from his reign) and 15 monasteries; he appointed royal sheriffs to uphold law and order in each district; he handed out charters recording the grants of land he had made to his knights, and the service owed in exchange. He declared vast tracts of land to be royal 'forest', where hunting (for food or sport) and fighting were banned. Mormaers were renamed 'counts' (a French noble title); a taoiseach became a chief.

King David also gave orders to build Scotland's first towns and mint Scotland's first coins. He appointed new bishops to organise priests and their congregations, and paid for new monasteries to spread the 'civilising' influence of the Roman Catholic Church.

Who were King David's newcomers? Some came from Norman France, which was the ancestral home of David's friends in the English ruling dynasty. Some came from England. Today, their names seem typically Scottish, but they all have English or French origins: Bruce, Comyn, Graham, Lindsay, Lyon, Melville, Menzies and many more, including perhaps the most famous Scottish name of all: Stewart.

These new Scots settled mostly in southern or central Scotland, fought in King David's army, organised his finances, ran his government, and built splendid castles to keep control of their new lands. Over the years they, too, became clan chiefs, as their own close family descendants multiplied, and as ordinary people living on their lands rented fields and cottages from them, fought alongside them against invaders, took their names and looked to them for protection. Just like the warlords' clans!

The Grahams: gallant or grim?

Ancient tradition claims that Clan Graham was descended from a Celtic tribesman called Grumach (the name means 'stern' or 'grim') who fought against the Romans. However, many historians think that the family of Graham was of Norman origin and first came to Scotland with David I. Sir William de Graham was recorded as witness to an important Scottish royal document in 1128. His descendants prospered, building up great estates in the rich lowlands of central Scotland. They also built up an impressive record of loyal service to Scottish kings, earning the nickname 'the Gallant Grahams'.

Clan Graham's greatest sons include:

* Sir Patrick, royal standard-bearer and the only Scots leader not to retreat at the Battle of Dunbar in 1296. He died there, fighting the English.

* Sir John, right-hand man of patriot William Wallace. He led his clansmen against the English in the victorious battle of Stirling Bridge (1297)

but was killed fighting alongside Wallace the next year, at the Battle of Falkirk.

* Sir David, one of the select group of Scottish nobles who signed the famous Declaration of Arbroath (sometimes called 'Scotland's Declaration of Independence') in 1320.

* A different Sir David, loyal supporter of Scottish hero Robert the Bruce (ruled 1306–1329).

* Another Sir John led a glorious but fatal charge against English archers at Neville's Cross near Durham in 1346.

* William, Lord Graham, died fighting the English at the Battle of Flodden Field in 1513.

* William Graham, 2nd Earl of Montrose, was one of the few Scots nobles to stay loyal to Mary Queen of Scots when she was deposed in 1568.

* John Graham, 3rd Earl of Montrose, was made Chancellor of Scotland by Mary's son, King James VI, in 1599.

❋ James Graham, 1st Marquess of Montrose ('The Great Montrose'), achieved Royalist victories during the Civil War in Scotland, from 1644. He was executed by Parliamentarians in 1650.

❋ John Graham, 7th Laird of Claverhouse, 1st Viscount Dundee ('Bonnie Dundee' to his friends, 'Bloody Clavers' to his enemies), led Jacobite armies to a famous victory at Killiecrankie in 1689, but died during the battle:

> To the Lords of Convention 'twas Claver'se
>   who spoke:
> 'Ere the King's crown shall fall there are crowns
>   to be broke;
> So let each Cavalier who loves honour and me,
> Come follow the bonnet of Bonny Dundee.
>
> *Chorus:*
> 'Come fill up my cup, come fill up my can,
> Come saddle your horses, and call up your men;
> Come open the West Port and let me gang free,
> And it's room for the bonnets of Bonny Dundee!'

Sir Walter Scott, 'Bonny Dundee', 1828–1829

Lords of Convention: members of a powerful assembly of Scottish nobles and church leaders.

Today, almost all the castles built by King David's new 'loyal lords' and the clans descended from them are in ruins. But several stirring stories about them still survive. Here are just a few:

Sheriff Stew

Castle: Glenbervie, Kincardineshire
Family: Melville

Sir John de Melville, the king's new sheriff, was a hard man, hated and feared by local clan leaders. Outraged by what they regarded as his attack on their ancient clan rights, they decided to take action.

Four, maybe five, of them invited Melville to a hunting party. Conveniently, they forgot to tell him that he would be the quarry! They chased him, captured him, boiled him alive – and then drank the broth together.

A deep hollow on a hill close to the castle is still known as the Sheriff's Kettle.

Earl Beardie

Castles: Finavon and Glamis (both in Angus)
Family: Lindsay

'Tiger' Lindsay, the 4th Earl of Crawford, was a brute of a man. Perhaps this was not entirely his fault; he came from a fierce family. He only inherited the title after his mother suffocated her own brother.

Also nicknamed 'Earl Beardie', 'Tiger' was famous – infamous – for dreadful deeds in two castles. At Finavon, his home, he hanged a minstrel on iron hooks for making a prophecy that came true: that the Lindsay family would be defeated in battle in 1452. Then he murdered messenger Jock Barefoot, for daring to cut a walking-stick from a mysterious ancient tree. He hanged poor Jock from the tree – now Jock's ghost haunts Finavon Castle.

At Glamis Castle, where he was a guest, Earl Beardie spent night after night playing cards. When warned not to play on the Sabbath, Earl Beardie flew into a furious rage. 'I'll play until Doomsday if I choose!' he roared. 'I'll even play with the Devil.' Suddenly a mysterious figure appeared and challenged Earl Beardie. The stakes for the game? The Earl's immortal soul against a sackful of rubies.

Of course, Earl Beardie played. Of course, he lost the wager. Of course he is doomed.

Doomed to play and lose at cards for ever – and to haunt Glamis.

The Mermaid's Song

Castle: Knockdolian, Ayrshire
Family: a branch of Clan Graham

How soft! How sweet! How charming! The sound of a beautiful mermaid, singing gently in the moonlight, as she reclines gracefully on a rock close to the castle walls.

Alas – that's not my lady of the castle's opinion. She can't stand the racket. It keeps her awake all night, she says. She's sending her servants to smash the rock; that dratted mermaid will have to go away.

And so she did, but not before singing a final verse:

> Ye may think on your cradle;
> I'll think on my stane,
> And there'll never be an heir
> To Knockdolian again.'

Quoted in Martin Coventry, *Castles of the Clans*,
Goblinshead 2008

stane: stone.

A curse! And it came true.

Beef for Bannocks!

Castle: Dunphail, Moray
Families: Comyn, Bruce

Two Norman-French families brought to Scotland by David I became bitter enemies: the Bruces and the Comyns. The feud began with a murder and continued for many years. In 1330, a chieftain from the Comyn family was besieged by members of the Bruce clan in Dunphail Castle. They had no food and little water; before long they were starving. Bravely, young Alastair Comyn, the chieftain's son, and four loyal companions managed to drag a sack of barley meal – used to make flat cakes, called *bannocks* – close to the castle, and to hurl it over the wall to the starving men inside.

It was a dark night, but even so, they were spotted, and tracked to their hiding place by a bloodhound. All five of them were beheaded. Their heads were thrown into the castle, just like the sack of meal, while the Bruce clansmen jeered: 'Here's beef for your bannocks!'

A man will die to save his honour.

Traditional Scottish saying

CHAPTER FOUR

MEANWHILE, IN THE HIGHLANDS AND ISLANDS…

In 1554 Queen Marie of Guise, regent for King David I's descendant, the glamorous, tragic, Mary Queen of Scots, visited the north of Scotland. She commanded Highland clan chiefs to meet her in Inverness. But MacKay of Farr refused. So Marie sent a loyal lord (and MacKay's sworn enemy), the Earl of Sutherland, to attack MacKay in his castle. It was captured and demolished, and MacKay himself was arrested.

Asked to produce the royal charters that proved his right to his clan lands, MacKay grabbed his dagger and slammed it down on his captors' table. *'Lamh laidir!'* he exclaimed, in Gaelic (say 'lamm lee-derr') – 'By my strong hand!'

Four hundred years before MacKay's dramatic gesture, King David I had 'planted' loyal knights on land around the northern and western borders of his Scottish kingdom. But, for all his grand ambitions, he knew that the wild terrain of northern Scotland and the even wilder seas around its coasts would make it impossible for him to control large areas of the Highlands and Islands.

David did what he could. He tried to make alliances with powerful Highland clan leaders. He tried to persuade or force them to swear allegiance to him. And he tried to use clan chiefs who had accepted his overlordship to keep control of the others. However, as MacKay's story shows, even 400 years later, not all were willing to accept royal authority (though the MacKays did ally with Scottish kings when fighting the English at the Battle of Bannockburn in 1314, for example). Throughout the Highlands and Islands, clan chiefs were in control.

Chiefs and people

Highland clan leaders played a part in national politics and international wars; they took sides in dynastic conflicts, winning power by supporting a successful claimant to the throne, or losing it by backing a failed one. They used diplomacy and brute force to increase clan landholdings or attract more clan members. There were frequent clashes along the boundaries between clan lands.

Within each clan territory, chiefs had tremendous powers: to collect tolls and taxes from their followers, hold markets, build and operate mills to grind grain, run law courts, and administer summary justice to criminals such as thieves. They held the dread power of *furca et fossa* (gallows and pit, for hanging men and drowning women) to punish serious crimes.

Rough justice

Dr Johnson relates the following tale:

In the Highlands it was a law, that if a robber was sheltered from justice, any man of the same clan might be taken in his place. This was a kind of irregular justice, which, though necessary in savage times, could hardly fail to end in a feud, and a feud once kindled among an idle people with no variety of pursuits to divert their thoughts, burnt on for ages either sullenly glowing in secret mischief, or openly blazing into public violence. Of the effects of this violent judicature, there are not wanting memorials.

The cave is now to be seen to which one of the Campbells, who had injured the MacDonalds, retired with a body of his own clan. The MacDonalds required the offender, and being refused, made a fire at the mouth of the cave, by which he and his adherents were suffocated together.

Samuel Johnson, *A Journey to the Western Islands of Scotland*, 1775

Clansmen were farmers, but also well-trained fighters; military virtues such as strength, courage and loyalty were highly prized. Violence was an accepted way of settling disputes, so death often came early. Even so, most clan conflict was small-scale and local, and directed at economic rather than human targets. Clans stole cattle (wealth literally 'on the hoof') or attacked property to drive rival clans from their homes. But for much of the time, many clans lived peacefully.

Family and followers

By King David I's time, clan members comprised two different kinds of people: the clan chiefs and their close kin (blood relatives), whose ancestry was known and recorded, and a large number of ordinary people, who 'belonged' to the clan in different ways. Some might be very distantly related to the chief's family, some might be servants or soldiers, some had actively sought the clan's protection; many were simply tenants, living on clan lands.

As we saw on page 43, clan leaders were also linked to clansfolk by the ancient custom of fostering. Chiefs' sons were sent to live with lower-ranking clan families for several years, to observe and learn. And, when times were hard, poor families might be persuaded by simple gifts of food to change their clan allegiance – and their name.

The Boll-Meal Frasers

Simon the Fox, 11th Lord Lovat and chief of Clan Fraser, was a staunch Jacobite. He wanted more men for his clan army, and so he offered a boll of oatmeal (about 140 lb or 63.5 kg; enough to feed a family for a winter) to any man willing to change his name and join the Fraser clan. Many poor men from families living close to the Fraser lands near Inverness accepted his offer. They were nicknamed the 'Boll-Meal Frasers'.

Simon Fraser led his clan – and his new recruits – in the Jacobite rebellion of 1745. Captured, and condemned to death in 1747, he was the last man to be beheaded at the Tower of London.

Who's who?

This example comes from the 1750s, but it records a custom that was older:

> John MackDonell...was really and truly a Campbell, having changed his name to that of MacDonell upon his coming to live in the bounds and under the protection of the family of Glengarry, it being the usual custom for those of a different name to take the name of the chieftain under whom they live.
>
> Gordon Donaldson, in *The Lyon in Mourning*, ed. Henry Paton , 1895, vol. III p. 152

Oh, to be able to travel back in time and ask the writer what he meant by the words 'really and truly a Campbell'! Probably, it was something like 'born and bred on Clan Campbell homelands'.

Founding fathers

From King David I's reign onwards, the real, historical founders of many Highland clans can be identified. For example, in the 'wild' Highlands, it seems likely that Murdo Cattanach (lived c.1150), a priest from Kingussie, was the ancestor of Clan MacPherson. Aed (pronounce 'Ay', as in 'say'), Earl of Moray, is said to have founded defiant Clan MacKay. The splendidly named Gillean ('Gill-layne' or 'Gill-lan') the Bloodaxe (died around 1250) is remembered as the originator of Clan MacLean, and Fergus, Lord of Galloway (lived some time between 1100 and 1200) was the ancestor of, yes, Clan Fergusson.

Among clans loyal to the monarchy, Clan Buchanan was said to descend from one Absalon, who was granted land by the king on the shores of Loch Lomond in 1225; Clan Boyd claimed descent from Simon, son of Sir Walter, the 6th hereditary High Steward (1296–1327).

A clan on the rise

Within the safe boundaries of the Scottish kingdom, the great Stewart family was descended from an earlier Sir Walter the Steward: Sir Walter Fitz Alan (d. 1177). He was the hereditary head of the royal household, chief tax collector and chief justice during the reign of David I.

After many generations of loyal service to the crown – and canny dynastic marriages – the Stewart family became kings and queens of Scotland from around 1371 to 1714.

Sir Walter was clearly a 'man of parts', as the Scots say. As well as founding a royal dynasty, he also won fame as a soldier. Aged only 21, he commanded the left wing of the victorious Scottish army at the Battle of Bannockburn, fought against the English, in 1314.

That sinking feeling...

Not all clan-origin stories from this era are entirely plausible, but they are ingenious and entertaining – which is why we remember them today. For example, in Gaelic, the name of Clan MacIntyre means 'son of the carpenter'. Traditionally, he was one MacArill, nephew to warlord Somerled (died c.1164), whom we met on page 14.

Clan MacIntyre's story tells how Somerled fell in love with Ragnhildis, daughter of the King of Man (who ruled the Isle of Man and several southern Scottish islands). The king would not agree to the marriage – until MacArill thought of a plan. Secretly, using his carpentry skills, MacArill made holes in the king's best warship. When the king set sail, seawater poured in; the king and his men were terrified.

But MacArill had concealed himself on board, along with a bundle of wooden bungs that he had carefully made beforehand. The carpenter struck a bargain with the king: 'Let my uncle marry your daughter, and I'll save your ship from sinking!' Ever since then, MacArill's descendants have been proud to be known as the 'Sons of the Carpenter'.

Somerled's sons

The history of Somerled's own descendants shows us how large clans with many branches might grow from one ancestor, in the Highlands or elsewhere. When Somerled died, he left three surviving sons: Dugald, Ranald and Angus. Their father's lands were divided between them, with the richest and most fertile going to Dugald, the eldest. Two of Somerled's sons became founders of three powerful new clans:

• Dugald: the MacDougalls

• Ranald: the MacDonalds (named after Ranald's son) and the MacRuaris (named after Ranald's grandson)

• Angus and his three sons were killed in a battle on Skye in 1200; his lands were shared between Ranald's sons.

After just five generations, Somerled's 'seed', all descended from him by blood, comprised four main clans and many lesser branches. Over the centuries these divided and sometimes joined together again, creating a kinship network of sometimes bewildering complexity that controlled most of the west coast of Scotland and the Hebrides.

Fair shares – and feuds

Somerled's sons each received a rich inheritance; but often the death of a clan chief led to fighting among his descendants. In the Highlands and Islands, either a living chief or the clan as a group nominated his next heir, the *tanaiste* (say 'taah-nish-te'). According to tradition, the best man was chosen for the task. It might be any one of the chief's sons, his brother, or even a cousin. Sons passed over for the honour might be sent with a few followers to find fresh places to conquer, or to live on marginal lands along the edges of clan territory. Once settled there, the new clan chief and his close kindred had to persuade the local people to follow them – and defend or win land along shifting clan boundaries.

Rí Innse Gall: Lord of the Isles

In 1156 Somerled defeated the Norse leader Godfrey the Black and took control of the islands off south and west Scotland. He also took over Godfrey's title: Lord of the Isles. Between 1163 and 1166, Somerled's MacDonald descendants took control of Skye and the northern Hebrides as well. MacDonald chiefs ruled their own private domain, safely out of reach of Scottish kings.

To keep control, the Lords of the Isles patrolled the seas around western Scotland with a fleet of *birlinn* (galleys – ships with sails and oars; their design evolved from earlier Viking warships). They collected tribute (or protection money) from clansmen and women living on their lands, and from surrounding chieftains.

Like any other ruler, the Lords of the Isles held a court, attended by their MacDonald 'royal' family, bodyguards, scribes, priests, warriors, poets, harpers and many other servants. They summoned 'royal' councils to their castle at Finlaggan on the isle of Islay; all the leading members of Clan Donald, and other friendly tribes, had to attend.

In 1493 King James IV of Scotland finally defeated the Lords of the Isles. But even before then, their power had been weakened by feuds between rival claimants to the chiefdom. These culminated in a sea fight between father and son: the Battle of Bloody Bay, fought close to Tobermory, on the Isle of Mull, around 1480.

Today the title Lord of the Isles belongs to Prince Charles, as the monarch's eldest son.

When in Scotland, Prince Charles is always known as the Duke of Rothesay – a title created in 1398 for members of the Stewart clan who had become kings of Scotland. Today it belongs to the heir apparent of the ruling monarch of the United Kingdom.

Better together

A few new, small or junior clans joined fortunes with other, unrelated clans, hoping to find mutual protection. The Clan Chattan confederation – proud motto: 'Touch not the cat but [without] a glove' – was formed some time after 1200. It included clans who lived amid some of Scotland's most majestic mountains, between Inverness and Braemar: Mackintosh, MacGillivray, MacBean, Shaw, MacThomas, MacLean of Dochgarroch, MacPherson, Farquharson, Davidson, MacPhail, MacQueen of Strathdearn, and one branch of the MacIntyre clan.

Without help from such a strong group of allies, small, weak clans risked being overpowered and turned off their clan lands. Today, Clan MacKinnon is closely linked to the Isle of Skye, but one branch, maybe more, originally lived on the Isle of Mull. When a young, inexperienced MacKinnon chief inherited these clan lands, the stronger neighbouring clan, MacLean of Duart, attacked and drove out the MacKinnon clansmen and their families.

The young chief sailed away to seek help from friends in Ireland and kin on Skye. This traditional tale tells what happened next:

The honour of Clan MacKinnon

Returning to Mull, young MacKinnon met an old woman – a witch! She told him that she could 'see' MacLean and his followers in a drunken stupor after feasting to celebrate their conquest of MacKinnon lands.

The young chief wasted no time. He rallied his followers and they each cut down a tall pine tree. They carried these trees to the house where drunken MacLean was still snoring, and planted them in the ground all around. Then young MacKinnon gently hung his sword in the open doorway, sharp point downwards. Silently, he led all his men away.

The next morning, MacLean and his men awoke – with terrible headaches – and saw the sword and the trees. They felt ashamed and extremely foolish. Their 'visitors' could have murdered them! Small, weak Clan

MacKinnon had won honour; the mighty MacLeans were disgraced.

Now the chief of Clan MacLean had to show that he, too, was worthy of respect. And he owed the MacKinnons a favour for not killing him and his men. A grand gesture was needed! He invited the MacKinnons to live on Mull once more, and promised never to attack them again.

As the MacKinnon story shows, sudden life-chances might raise – or lower – the fortunes of whole clan: a young or daring chief, a murder, a defeat in war, a lack of male heirs, quarrels between fathers and sons, fights among brothers, or a marriage.

The Campbells are coming!

The Campbells are comin, Oho, Oho!
The Campbells are comin, Oho, Oho!
The Campbells are comin to bonie Lochleven,
The Campbells are comin, Oho, Oho!

Robert Burns, 'The Campbells are Coming', 1790
(adapted from a Jacobite song of 1715)

Besides the MacDonalds, other large and successful Highland clans included the Campbells, who lived among the hills and lochs of Argyll on the southern edge of the Highlands, and the MacKenzies, whose home was in the bleak, rugged moors and mountains of Ross.

The Campbells first won power through the friendship of their chief, Niall, with Robert the Bruce. A famous warrior, Bruce was descended from an Anglo-Norman knight, and his mother was the great-great granddaughter of King David I. In 1290, Bruce claimed to be the rightful heir to the Scottish throne after King Alexander III and his 6-year-old heiress, the Maid of Norway, both died.

To cut a long story brutally short, Bruce became King Robert I in 1306, and the Campbells were rewarded with large amounts of land taken from their neighbours and enemies, the MacDougalls. Chiefs of Clan MacDougall (see page 73) were allies of, and closely related to, Bruce's great rival for the throne, John Balliol.

Two generations later, Campbell chief Gilleasbuig (say 'Gillespie' or 'Gillespic'; died c.1387) won further vast estates in the west. For extra security, he befriended neighbouring noble Robert Stewart, who became King Robert II in 1371. This friendship was also richly rewarded: the Campbells were made hereditary royal lieutenants in the southwest Highlands, and by 1395 they were calling themselves 'Lords of Argyll'.

A further century later, through marriage, by service as royal courtiers, and by fighting for the king against the MacDonalds, a Campbell chief achieved the highest position in the royal government, Lord Chancellor, in 1483.

Unquiet souls

The Campbells' imposing fortress at Inverary is said to be haunted – by flocks of long-dead ravens, by a murdered servant and a plaintive harper, and by a ghostly ship that appears when a member of the Campbell family is about to die.

The unspeakable truth

Coinneach Odher (say 'Keanoch Ower'), born on the Isle of Lewis around 1650, was said to have second sight. He went to work at Brahan castle, near Dingwall, home of the chief of Clan Mackenzie. The chief was away in France, and Lady MacKenzie asked Coinneach Odher to use his powers to check that her husband was safe. The Seer looked, and saw, and spoke: 'His Lordship does very well.' The Lady wanted more news. At first the Seer refused, but she insisted. The Brahan Seer could only speak the truth, and it had been better left unsaid. His Lordship was dallying with a pretty Frenchwoman. Her Ladyship, outraged, had the Seer burnt to death in a barrel of boiling tar.

Northern lords

Further north, Clan MacKenzie, based in Kintail (the mainland opposite the Isle of Skye), began their rise to power after helping the armies of King Alexander III to defeat King Håkon Håkonsson of Norway at the Battle of Largs in 1263.

Until then, Norwegians had ruled the islands all along Scotland's west coast, from the Isle of Man and the Kintyre peninsula to the northernmost tip of the Hebrides. As a reward for fighting against them, the MacKenzie chiefs were given the splendid fortress known as Eilean Donan Castle by the king. That became the MacKenzie base for expansion to the east and north; by around 1600, the MacKenzies controlled all Ross-shire. Scottish hero Robert the Bruce hid in Eilean Donan in 1306; criminals' heads used to be displayed on ghastly spikes around its walls. Today the castle is said to be haunted – by a ghost who carries his head under his arm.

"

Cnuic is uillt is Ailpeinich

Hills and streams and MacAlpins

From an old Gaelic rhyme

"

CHAPTER FIVE

HOME GROUND

When clansmen charged into battle, the air was thick not only with the clash of sword against sword, the skirl and shriek of the pipes, and the moans of the dying, but also with the slogans (Gaelic *sluagh-ghairm*, war cry) shouted by the warriors on each side. The Grants, for example, yelled, 'Stand Fast, Craigellachie!' (Craigellachie was a landmark hill beside the River Spey in the Highlands.) Clan MacDonald roared 'Heathery Isle!'

In spite of Scottish kings, each clan claimed its *dùthchas* (ancestral homeland). Some, like the MacAlpins, liked to think that they had lived there from the beginning of the world; they belonged there naturally, like the trees and the heather. A comforting sentiment, but the reality was rather different. As one clan grew stronger, others grew weaker, and Scotland's land changed hands over and over again. The geography of power was shifting all the time.

Even so, land was vitally important to all Scottish clans. Without land, a clan was nothing. A landless clan was said to be 'broken'; in the same way, a man without a clan was a 'broken man'. Chiefs, clansmen and clanswomen identified with their clan community. Land sustained and supported a whole clan.

More land meant more wealth, more produce and more power. Even more important, land meant more people: a bigger, stronger, more numerous clan. The greater the number of families a chief could settle on his land, the more potential soldiers and servants he had. New clan members increased his wealth, because everyone had to pay rent, usually in food, for the lands they occupied. Adult males also had to serve in his army. As late as the

18th century, chief MacDonell of Keppoch described his rentbook as '500 fighting men'.

Forced 'gifts'

Until 1609 (see pages 143–144) chiefs could demand food and lodgings for their soldiers and servants in tenants' homes (this could leave a family hungry for months), together with 'gifts' such as a share of colts, calves and lambs born on clan lands, and even, in the Islands, the right to take one child out of each pair of twins.

Traditionally, these payments and services were described as *cuid oidiche* (say 'kujj eech-yah'), the duty of hospitality owed by clansmen and women to the head of their 'family'. Even so, chiefs did not rely on their tenants' finer feelings. They kept detailed records of the payments in produce or money due to them from clan lands.

Am baile: Life in a clan township

Clan families lived as self-sufficient subsistence farmers, in small, clustered settlements known as *bailtean* (townships; say 'bal-chun'). They paid rent to their clan chief in kind: grain, livestock or 'reeking hens' (chickens from each house where a fire was burning – that is, each inhabited house). They also had to do farmwork for him.

Houses were low, dark, smoky and very small – some no more than 4 x 2 m (13 x 6½ ft); they might be made of slabs of turf, or rough stone and rammed earth, or wattle (interwoven branches). They were thatched with heather, dried grass or bracken, which might last for only a few seasons. There might be a small kailyard (vegetable patch) close beside each dwelling.

Scarce, valuable arable land – the *inbye* – surrounded each township. This was laid out in strips, in small open fields protected by low turf walls. Families each had a share of good and poor land; the system of dividing and apportioning was known as *runrig*. Most farmwork was done by hand: men dug the ground using a simple wooden foot-plough; men and women carried baskets of seaweed, sand, peat, old thatch and cattle manure to fertilise thin, poor, stony soils. Everyone worked together to gather the harvest; the chief crops were oats and bere (barley).

Each township also had an area of rough *outbye* land beyond the fields. This was used for grazing sheep, goats or cattle in winter, and occasionally might be ploughed to grow grain. Beyond this, the township had access to rough common pasture – often on steep hillsides, or beside the sea, or in marshy ground. Families let their few precious animals graze freely there. For a few weeks in summer, young women might lead the family cows up to high summer pastures. There they would shelter in *sheilings* (rough huts), making butter and cheese from summer milk to last all winter.

If families lived by the sea, they might catch fish or seabirds to eat, or gather shellfish. Inland, there were salmon and trout in rivers, and hare and wild birds on the mountains; but chiefs, and later landlords, claimed all rights to hunt on clan land. Most clansmen and women survived on a diet of oats, milk, butter, cheese, cabbage, and a few eggs and wild berries.

Rich and poor

Law courts also kept records of individual clansmen's and women's possessions when they died. Some of the earliest that we have, from the late 17th century, show that there could be a considerable difference in wealth between clan members – and that some were desperately poor.

Agnes McDonald, 25 September 1694

60 great cows, 12 young cows; 12 bullocks, 8 horses and mares with their foals, 20 sheep and goats; 8 bolls corn; household food stores.
Debts owing to deceased: over £100 by cattle-drover
Debts owed by deceased: servants' fees £20; funeral £20

Margaret NcLain, 3 December 1700

5 cows, 1 old mare, corn sown in the ground (may yield 1 boll)
'Extraordinary poor'

Source: http://www.moidart.org.uk/datasets/
argyllinventory.htm

Nc: short for Nic, 'daughter of'; 1 boll: approx. 140 lb (63.5 kg) dry weight.

Tacks and rent

A clan chief and his family could not oversee every last corner of clan lands. Instead, they relied on *tacksmen*. A *tack* was a lease on an area of land; tacksmen might be junior members of the chief's kin, or senior, trusted, prosperous members of the wider clan community. Each tack covered a separate area of clan territory; the tacksman paid rent for it to the chief, and sublet portions of it to ordinary men and women, either townships (small clusters of houses and byres) or individual cottages.

The white cow

Members of Clan MacIntyre tell a story about homeland, and rent:

After clan founder MacArill the Carpenter was safely back on dry land (see pages 72–73), he and his descendants were advised in a dream to make their homeland where the only white cow among their herd decided to sit down and rest. She chose well: sheltered, fertile Glen Noe, beside beautiful Loch Etive. At first, MacArill and his men were able to fight off all attackers, but later they put themselves under the protection of their powerful neighbours, Clan Campbell.

The rent they paid was unusual, but full of symbolic meaning: a fine fat calf at Christmas from the sweet grasslands of the glen, and a snowball at midsummer from the corries (high hollows) at the top of forbidding Ben Cruachan, a mountain that marked the southern border of the MacIntyre lands.

If the MacIntyres could revisit Ben Cruachan today, they might be very surprised to find that the whole mountain has been hollowed out to house a massive hydroelectric power station.

Names and places

Clansmen and women identified themselves by their ancestry and also their home location. Their own private history was embedded in their name: 'Angus son of Donald son of Iain' or 'Mary daughter of Hugh son of Duncan son of James'. Descent was patrilineal – traced through men. Many personal names came from places: Calum Ross ('of the headland'), Allan Blair ('of the field'), Marsaili Craig ('of the rock'). Nicknames were common, such as 'Big Donald', 'Young Alasdair' or 'Red Anna'.

Group identity

Clan names were mostly only used by outsiders, when speaking of clansfolk as a group: 'Those lawless MacDonalds!' 'Those miserable MacKenzies!' Clan members were known by the name of their clan chief, whether or not they were related to him, or to each other.

As we have seen, clans were often named after an ancient, heroic founder – perhaps with distinctive characteristics, such as Cameron (*cam sron*, 'crooked nose'), Campbell (*cam beul*, 'twisted mouth', or perhaps 'liar'), Grant (French *grand*, 'big') or MacBain (*bheathain*, 'lively one'). Other clans took their name from their 'seat' (centre of power; often the site of the chief's strongest castle), for example Douglas (*dubh glas*, 'black water'), Innes (*innis*, 'island'), Dunlop (*dun*, 'fort' or 'hill', plus *lob*, 'mud'). Gow (*gobhan*, 'blacksmith'), MacBrayne (*mac mreithearch*, 'son of the judge'), Lamont ('lawman') and MacSporran ('purse-bearer') are occupational names; MacMillan, MacPherson and Malcolm all mean 'son or servant of a priest'.

Men and land

The chief of a clan was known by his family name – 'The MacDonald' – but heads of all the junior branches were named after the areas of territory they controlled, such as MacDonell of Keppoch, Campbell of Cawdor, Stewart of Appin and Brodie of Brodie. They were addressed by the place name – 'Appin', 'Brodie' – not their clan name.

If a clan chief lived at the family seat, in the centre of clan homelands, he might be referred to as 'of that ilk'. In the Scots language, *ilk* means 'the same', or 'that kind' or 'that type'.

A name to conjure with

Chiefs knew their ancestry right back to the founders of their clan:

Alasduir
Mic Ragnuill
Mhic Dhonaill Glais
Mhic Aonguis
Mhic Alasduir Charraich
Mhic Eoin
Mhic Aonguis Og

Alasdair, chief of clan MacDonell of Keppoch, 1616, and seven generations of his ancestors, as reported, in Gaelic, in the *Celtic Magazine*, 1879

Mic: an old spelling of Mac, 'son'. For women, the equivalent is Nighean, *(pronounced 'nean'), 'daughter', or, in some old documents,* Nic.

Mhic, pronounced 'vic': the possessive form of Mac.

"

This I'll defend!

Motto, Clan MacFarlane

Buaidh no bas!

Victory or death

War cry, Clan MacNeill

Danger is sweet

Motto, Clan MacAulay

Endure with strength

Motto, Clan Lindsay

"

CHAPTER SIX

BONNIE FECHTERS

Red Harlaw! The very mention of that clash between clans sends a shudder down the spine. Awarded its gruesome nickname because so much blood was shed, the Battle of Harlaw was fought in 1411 between the followers of two rival clan chiefs: Robert Stewart, Duke of Albany, and Donald, Lord of the Isles. Both men wanted the rich earldom of Ross. The brutality of the fighting soon passed into Scottish folklore. Much later, it became the subject of a popular ballad, probably composed around 1600.

On Monanday, at mornin,
The battle it began,
On Saturday, at gloamin,
Ye'd scarce kent wha had wan.

An sic a weary buryin
I'm sure ye never saw
As wis the Sunday after that,
On the muirs aneath Harlaw.

Gin ony body speer at you
For them ye took awa,
Ye may tell their wives and bairnies
They're sleepin at Harlaw.

From F. J. Child, *The English and Scottish
Popular Ballads*, 1882–1898, no. 163

*gloamin: dusk, evening; kent: known; wha: who;
wan: won; sic: such; wis: was; muirs aneath:
moors below; Gin ony: if any; speer at: ask;
awa: away; bairnies: children.*

In reality the fighting only lasted one day, not
six. It just felt as if it went on for ever.

The 'red' battle of Harlaw was part of a long
dispute over inheritance. It belonged to a
tradition of fighting for kin-based land and

rank that stretched back for hundreds of years. Even kings took part. In one particularly shocking example, King Alexander II (died 1249) had ordered the public execution of a baby girl, the last surviving member of the MacWilliam kindred. Her relatives, his rivals, had claimed descent from Scottish kings, and led an unsuccessful rebellion in a bid to take over royal power. As a contemporary chronicler reported:

> Mac-William's daughter, who had not long left her mother's womb, innocent as she was, was put to death, in the burgh of Forfar, in view of the market place, after a proclamation by the public crier. Her head was struck against the column of the market cross, and her brains dashed out.

From the Lanercost Chronicle, compiled 1272–1346

Even for the often violent times in which he lived, King Alexander seems exceptionally ruthless. Eight years earlier, he had ordered that 80 men from Caithness should have their hands and feet cut off in punishment for roasting the local bishop alive.

Weapons and tactics

Throughout the 'Age of the Clans' (from around 1100 to 1500) conflicts ranged all the way from minor skirmishes – when a few clansmen ambushed travellers from an enemy clan, or raided an isolated township, or drove away cattle – to full-scale pitched battles like Harlaw.

In a typical battle, clansmen lined up in tight ranks two or three deep, side by side, facing their opponents. Chiefs wore heavy coats of chainmail (replaced by plate armour from around 1500) and metal helmets; ordinary clansmen wore thickly padded tunics coated with pitch, or stout leather jerkins. Each man was armed with a spear and a small round targe (shield). From around 1400, clansmen also slashed and stabbed at their enemies with fearsome 'Lochaber axes' – hooked blades on long poles. Similar pikes were used elsewhere, especially in the Borders. Scottish chiefs and chieftains had horses. Cattle raiders rode small, tough ponies. But otherwise, clans fought on foot, continuing the traditions of earlier Viking and Pictish warriors.

When the massed ranks of clansmen were ready, they charged. With luck on their side, the shock of their attack would force the enemy to scatter; after this, the clansmen could pick off individual foes. Clan slogans (see page 85) were shouted to encourage or regroup the clansmen, and to call for urgent assistance. Occasionally, clans continued ancient Celtic traditions of warfare, such as cutting off the heads of slaughtered enemies.

After around 1600, guns (chiefly muskets), axes and swords replaced spears, and bows and arrows became more popular. Clansmen now charged to within gunshot-distance of the enemy (very roughly, about 50–70 yards/ 45–65 metres), fired one volley to break their opponents' ranks, then rushed on to engage in hand-to-hand fighting. Speed, strength and agility on foot remained just as important.

In the words of the motto of Clan MacKinnon:

Fortune assists the brave.

A terrible trophy

Clan Grant and Clan Comyn were fighting – and Clan Grant gained the upper hand. Grant clansmen swarmed into the Comyn castle, seized the Comyn chief and killed him.

The dead chief's head was taken back to the Grant castle and cleaned; the skull was kept as a memorial of a famous battle. Centuries later, visitors to the castle reported that a neat, hinged flap had been made in the top of the skull, and that documents were kept inside.

According to Clan Grant tradition, if the skull ever leaves the Grant chief's family, the clan will lose all its lands in Strathspey.

102

Death before dishonour

Loyalty to a leader was all-important. Members of Clan MacAlister proudly tell this story:

In 1614 the chief of Clan Campbell, the earl of Argyll, led his men to attack the MacDonalds of Islay. Soldiers from the MacAlisters, a much smaller, weaker clan, were among the Campbell troops. Because of an earlier agreement made between MacAlister and a Campbell chief, the Campbells had the right to summon MacAlister clansmen to fight for them.

However, by ancestry the MacAlister chiefs had ancient ties with the chiefs of Clan MacDonald. They, too, were descended from Somerled; they were kin. As a weak, junior branch of the huge MacDonald clan, they regarded the MacDonald chief as the head of their family, and as their ultimate leader.

The MacAlisters marched and sailed with the Campbells to Islay. But as soon as battle began, the MacAlister chief led his clansmen to change sides and join the MacDonalds –

and they followed him. This proved the loyalty of both chief and men, but it was also suicidal: even without the MacAlisters, the Campbells were stronger. Many, many MacAlister clansmen died in the fighting. The MacAlister chief and MacDonald of Islay were both captured – and executed.

It is, however, only fair to add that some clan chiefs' armies contained many mercenary troops – professional soldiers who would fight for anyone who paid them. It was rumoured that the MacDonald army at Harlaw was boosted by up to 10,000 Irish mercenaries.

Paid or unpaid, not to fight 'like a man' was a matter of deep disgrace and dishonour. Shortly after 1700, men from Clan MacDonald of Glencoe attacked a party of MacPhersons. Most of their victims who stood and fought back were left dead or dying. But a few MacPhersons escaped and reached home safely – only to be met with stern disapproval. They were punished by being made to walk round and round the local church, carrying shameful wooden swords and confessing: 'We are the cowards who ran away.'

Culloden Moor
(Seen in Autumn Rain)

The Battle of Culloden was fought in 1746 between armies loyal to the British government, and Scottish clansmen and others who supported Jacobite claimants to the British throne. Many claim that Culloden was 'the end of the clans'.

Full of grief, the low winds sweep
O'er the sorrow-haunted ground;
Dark the woods where night rains weep,
Dark the hills that watch around.

. . .

Here that broken, weary band
Met the ruthless foe's array,
Where those moss-grown boulders stand,
On that dark and fatal day.

. . .

Noble dead that sleep below,
We your valour ne'er forget;
Soft the heroes' rest who know
Hearts like theirs are beating yet.

Alice McDonell of Keppoch, 1855–1938

Siege warfare

The Campbell–MacDonald clash described on pages 103–104 was a siege, at Dunnyveg Castle. During sieges, attacking soldiers surrounded a castle – or a mountain hideout – trying to smash through its walls or shoot and kill the defenders sheltering inside. Sometimes besiegers lit fires at the base of castle walls, hoping that the heat might crack the stonework and drive out the defenders. Besieging troops also did their best to prevent fresh food from reaching the castle, and polluted or poisoned water supplies. Defenders trapped by a siege might die of starvation, or succumb to disease. If their attackers gained entry, they either fought to the death or were forced to surrender.

Call to arms

Clan armies were famously summoned by the 'fiery cross' – two wooden sticks tied together by a bloody rag, and carried from township to township by a swift runner. As well as snatching up their weapons at first sight of the signal, clansmen would also grab a sprig of their clan emblem, a local plant such as heather or Scots pine. This was partly to wear in their bonnets as a badge of identity, and partly also for magical protection.

The fiery cross was copied – alas – by the disgraceful Ku Klux Klan in the USA.

Magic forces

As well as protective emblems, many clans also had talismans. One of the most famous was the Clach na Bratach (Banner-Stone), a ball of rock crystal which belonged to Clan Robertson. It was carried into battle by Robertson chiefs to give them strength and courage. It was said to have healing powers; when placed in water, its ability to cure passed into that, as well. Rather more worryingly, it was also believed to foresee the future, and to warn (by turning cloudy) whenever a chief of Clan Robertson was going to die. When it cracked, as it did before the Jacobite rebellion of 1715, that foretold disaster!

Chiefs, crests and badges

Heraldic crests made clan chiefs easy to identify, even in armour. Their followers wore copies of these crests, stamped or cast on metal plates, on a leather strap buckled across the chest. Smaller versions, surrounded by belt and buckle, were later worn as badges. Here are just a few:

Bruce Standing lion

Campbell Boar's head

Chisholm Hand holding dagger with boar's head impaled.

Colquhoun Hart's (young male deer's) head

Douglas Salamander (magic lizard) in fire

Drummond Goshawk perched on coronet

Ferguson Bee on thistle

Graham Eagle attacking stork

Grant (also **MacKenzie**) Mountain in flames

Livingstone Half-naked man holding a club, with a snake around his arm.

MacDougall Right arm in armour holding dagger

MacDuff Top half of lion holding dagger

MacGregor Lion's head, crowned

Urquhart Woman holding sword and tree

Wallace Right arm in armour, holding sword

Seventeenth-century traveller Martin Martin (see page 118) recorded another magic ritual:

> When any chieftain marched upon a military expedition [he would]…draw some blood from the first animal that chanced to meet them on the enemy's ground, and sprinkle it on his army's banners. This was believed to be an omen of future success.

Clan warriors often strengthened the bond between them by becoming blood-brothers: they drank a few drops of each other's blood. (Readers, we're sure you know well enough not to try this at home.)

War without end

With death so clearly in prospect, why did clansmen fight? For land, for cattle, for clan – and for honour. Many conflicts began as minor skirmishes, but soon escalated into clan feuds that carried over from one generation to the next and caused widespread, wasteful destruction. In order not to lose their proud reputation, chiefs and clansmen felt compelled to take part.

Here is part of an account, written in the 18th century, of a long feud between the Macleans and the MacDonalds. The fighting described took place around 1590:

Angus Macdonald, returning out of Ireland... with a great preparation of men and shipping he went into the islands and Tiree appertaining to Maclean, invading these places with great hostility; where, what by fire, what by sword, and what by water, he destroyed all the men that he could overtake (none excepted), and all sorts of beasts that served for domestic use and pleasure of man; and, finally, came to the very Ben Mor, in Mull, and there killed and chased the Clan Lean at his pleasure, and so fully revenged himself of his former injuries.

Whilst Angus Macdonald was thus raging in Mull and Tiree, Sir Lauchlan Maclean went into Kintyre, spoiled, wasted, and burnt a great part of that country; and thus, for a while, they did continually vex one another with slaughters and outrages, to the destruction, well near, of all their country and people.

Quoted in Alexander MacGregor,
The Feuds of the Clans [1907], pp. 94–95

Going at it hammer and tongs?

Feuds were not just murderous and wasteful, but also a threat to the security of the Scottish kingdom. In 1396 King Robert III took drastic steps to try to end a long-running, 'bold and barbarous' quarrel between Clan Kay and Clan Chattan.

Robert commanded that 30 men should be chosen from each clan to fight and settle the quarrel once and for all. The combatants, armed with swords, were assembled on a level field in the city of Perth, close to the River Tay. The king and his nobles were spectators.

It was time for the battle to start – but one warrior from Clan Chattan ran off, overcome with terror. No other clansman was willing to stand in for him; no man from Clan Kay would withdraw to make both sides equal, for fear that he would be shamed as a coward.

Must the whole contest be abandoned? For a long while, it seemed so. At last, a blacksmith, Henry Wynd, stepped forward. He would fight and risk his life, he said, in return for a French crown (a coin) of pure gold. To a working man, that was a fortune.

The king gave a sign! The heralds blew their trumpets! The clansmen hurled themselves at each other! Both sides fought with 'inconceivable fury', but, thanks in no small part to the strength and courage of Henry Wynd, Clan Chattan were victorious. Of all their clansmen who fought, only ten survived, and all were badly injured. All the Clan Kay fighters were killed, except one, who escaped by swimming across the river. And Henry Wynd got his money.

Keeping it in the family

Rival factions within clans also feuded. Today, a famous monument stands beside the main road from Inverness to Fort William. It has a sinister name: the Well of the Seven Heads.

In 1663 the young chieftain MacDonell of Keppoch and his brother were murdered. The killers were their jealous uncle and his six sons. For a while the killers went free, but in 1665 the Edinburgh government gave permission for the murdered men's relatives to act against them, with 'ample and summary vengeance'. A war party of sixty raided their house. The uncle and his sons were beheaded.

MacDonell clan poet Iain Lom took the bloody, dripping heads to show the local Clan Donald chief, MacDonell of Glengarry. On the way, he stopped to wash them at a nearby spring – and instantly gave it a new name. The monument that travellers see today was commissioned by Colonel MacDonell of Glengarry in 1812.

Wild reivers

Much further south, in the wild, rugged uplands of the Scottish Borders, clans such as the Armstrongs, Maxwells, Nixons, Kerrs, Elliots and Johnstons bravely fought English invaders from before 1300 well into the 1500s. They also made a living by feuding and *reiving* (raiding). Rich or poor, clan chief or humble clansman, the reivers rode out on fast, sure-footed horses called 'hobblers'. Their aim?

To snatch money or goods from remote farmsteads or, just as important, to drive away valuable beef cattle, sheep and goats. Reivers also extorted protection money, known as 'blackmail' – *mail* being a Scots word for 'rent', here used ironically. (That's where the modern word originated.)

Leaders of reiver gangs were given as much respect as the grandest Highland clan chiefs. One of the most famous was 'Kinmount Willie' Armstrong. Apprehended by a cruel, unlawful trick in 1596, he was sprung from prison by his allies and never recaptured.

In the same year, Geordie Burn was caught red-handed while driving home stolen cattle. Before his execution he made an (alleged) confession, stating that he had:

> lain with above forty men's wives…killed seven Englishmen with his own hand, cruelly murdering them…spent his whole time in whoring, drinking, stealing and taking deep revenge for slight offences.

Source: http://www.historicuk.com/HistoryUK/
Scotland-History/BorderReivers.htm

Almost certainly, this was negative propaganda, spread by Geordie's enemies in a bid to smear his name.

The power of the Border reiving clans faded after 1605, when King James VI and I sent out Border Commissioners to bring law and order. In their very first year they hanged 79 reivers.

One of Kinmount Willie's most famous exploits was a daring ride to escape his pursuers, across the River Eden:

> He is either himsel' or a devil frae hell
> Or else his mother a witch maun be;
> I wadna hae ridden that wan water,
> For a' the gow in Christendie.

Sir Walter Scott, *Minstrelsy of the Scottish Borders*, 1802–1803

frae: from; maun: must; wadna hae: wouldn't have; gow: gold.

66

Anywhere where The MacDonald sits is the head of the table.

Allegedly said by a great clan chief when his host's servants apologised for seating him far away from the place of honour at the head of the table

99

WEALTH AND PRIDE

P icture the scene. It's somewhere in the Western Isles, some time before 1650. A young man has climbed up to the top of a pyramid-shaped heap of stones, and is standing there with his father's sword in one hand and a white stick in the other. The base of the pyramid is ringed by a group of men and women. And a man with a loud voice is chanting, chanting, chanting...

What is going on?

What we are witnessing is a traditional ceremony for installing a new clan chief. It was described by Martin Martin, the son of a prosperous tacksman on Skye, around 1695. Martin adds that, before the new young chief could be acclaimed by his clan followers, he would have to prove his valour by leading a party of 'young men of quality' who had not yet seen action on a successful raid to attack a neighbouring clan. They had to bring back the cattle they found there, 'or die in the attempt'.

Raids like this were not considered crimes by clansmen and women; they were ways in which power struggles between clans could be settled without too much bloodshed, and they allowed young chiefs and the clans they led to bid for attention and make their mark.

'Let us now praise famous men'

Here are the closing lines of the *Duan Albanach*, a long poem praising Scottish kings and their ancestors, written during the reign of Kenneth MacAlpin's great-great-great grandson, Malcolm III (ruled 1058–1093). Similar poems would have been sung at the installation of new chiefs.

Six years, Donnchad the wise,
Seventeen years, the son of Fionnlaoch;
After Macbeathadh, the renowned,
Seven months in the lordship, Luglaigh.

Maolcoluim is now the king,
Son of Donnchad, the florid of lively visage,
His duration knoweth no man
But the wise one, the most wise,
        O ye learned.

Quoted in William F. Skene, *Chronicles of the Picts, Chronicles of the Scots, and Other Early Memorials of Scottish History*, 1867

(Macbeathadh, son of Fionnlaoch, is the original of Shakespeare's Macbeth; Donnchad and Maolcoluim are Shakespeare's King Duncan and his son Malcolm.)

Chief, chieftain, captain, laird...

What's the difference?

* A **chief** was the head of the senior (oldest) branch of any clan, and could be a man or a woman – although in the warlike Age of the Clans, a man was very much preferred. The chief was addressed by the name of his or her clan: The Campbell, The Fraser. A woman chief always used her own clan name, not her husband's. Chiefs were also known as the 'son of' their clan's real or legendary founder: for example, the chief of Clan Campbell was 'MacCailean Mor' (Big Colin's son).

Technically, in Scottish law, a chief is the 'chief of the name and arms' of, for example, MacGregor or MacTavish. The name and coat of arms have a protected legal status; the clan is a social, not a legal, institution.

The rank and title of chief passed from father to legitimate son. 'Legitimate' normally meant 'son of a lawful wedded wife', but in Scotland children of traditional informal marriages were also recognised. Historians sometimes call these arrangements 'secular Celtic' marriages. They could result – as in one case from the 15th century – in a father having six legitimate sons, all from different mothers.

* A **chieftain** was the head of a junior (younger) branch, or *sept*. Chieftains were addressed by the name of their land, for example Cawdor, Clanranald. In the past, they were sometimes called 'the chieftain of the countrie'.

* A **captain** was not a clan chief, though he was often closely related. He might be appointed to act as leader in a difficult situation (if the clan chief was imprisoned, for example), or for one battle-campaign, or to command several different septs or small clans working or fighting together, as in the case of 'The Captain of Chattan'.

* A **laird** (Scots for 'lord') was a high-ranking man owning a large amount of land, and living on it – not necessarily a clan leader. The title was sometimes used to refer to a clan chief or chieftain.

* A **tanaiste** was a near relative of a clan chief who was recognised as his next heir. He was selected – sometimes only after conflict – from close kin, because he was the most capable candidate. This might be necessary if, for example, a dead chief's son and heir was too young to rule or fight, or if the chief had no suitable heirs.

Some other titles

* The eldest son and heir of a chief is called by his own first name and his clan surname, together with his father's territorial designation, plus the abbreviation 'yr' for 'younger': Donald MacKay of Farr, yr.

* The wife of a clan chief or chieftain (or his heir) may choose to be called 'Madam': Madam MacGregor of MacGregor, or Madam Douglas of Drumlanrig. If her husband has a title, she will use the female counterpart, instead, e.g. Lady MacDonald of the Isles.

* The eldest daughter of the chief of Clan MacDougall is known as The Maid of Lorn.

Keeping up appearances

A chief was the 'Representer' of the illustrious ancestor who was said to have founded the clan. As such, he was entitled to great respect; he also felt it his duty to put on a brave and lavish display, for the honour and glory of the clan kindred and all its followers. The grander the chief, the greater the clan.

When a chief goes on a journey in the hills, or makes a formal visit to an equal, he is said to be attended by all, or most part of the officers following viz.

The henchmen (bodyguard)…
Bard His poet
Bladier His spokesman
Gilli-more Carries his broadsword
Gilli-casflue Carries him on foot, over the fords
Gilly-constraine Leads his horse on rough and dangerous way
Gilly-trusharnarish The baggage man
The piper Who being a gentleman, I should have mentioned sooner
And lastly,
The pipers Gilly Who carries the bagpipes

There are likewise some gentlemen near of his kin who bear him company, and besides a number of the common sort, who have no particular employment, but follow him only to partake of the cheer.

Quoted in John Jamieson, *An Etymological Dictionary of the Scottish Language*, Supplement, vol. 1, 1825, pp. 478–479

Trained to please

According to Martin Martin (see page 118), the 'competent number of young men' who accompanied a clan chief were well trained in swordfighting as well as 'wrestling, swimming, jumping, dancing, shooting with bows and arrows'. And they were proficient sailors. Chiefs also paid for the services of many hereditary officials, from bards to pipers, harpers, gatekeepers, nightwatchmen, purse-carriers, foresters and huntsmen. These men often had the right to be paid in food or clothing by the chief's tenants; the MacDonald quartermaster was given cattle-hides; the lord's gallowglass (tough bodyguard; the same name was also used for clansmen who travelled to Ireland and continental Europe to fight as mercenaries) received double portions of meat to keep him strong.

Just like loyal Anglo-Norman lords (see page 53), clan chiefs in areas outside the control of Scottish kings built forts and castles. These combined strength and protection with defiant boastfulness. Castles ranged from tall, forbidding tower-houses and peel towers (in the Borders) to large castles of enclosure, with a thick outer curtain wall sheltering timber-framed, and later stone, living quarters inside.

Naturally, such larger-than-life buildings attracted tales of mystery and magic; for example, Dun Sgathaich castle (say 'Dun Sky-ah' or 'Dun Scaith'), on the Isle of Skye, was reputed to have been built by a witch. Duntulm Castle, in the north of the same island, was said to be haunted by pirate outlaw Hugh MacDonald, who was imprisoned and left to die horribly, with lots of salted beef but no water, and by Margaret MacLeod, bride of a MacDonald chief. When she lost one of her eyes in an accident, her husband threw her out, with only a one-eyed servant to attend her, and a one-eyed horse, and a one-eyed dog.

See and wonder!

In wild, rugged, unproductive areas such as Highland Scotland, control of land equalled control of food – and control of food equalled control of life itself. Perhaps one harvest in every three in the bleak Highlands and Islands failed, and led to scarcity. And springtime was always a hungry season.

In such grim circumstances, the head of a clan became the provider for all his people, by redistributing, as emergency aid, some of the food payments he had received in tribute. He stored produce in his *girnal houses* (barns) to provide food for the starving, but also used some of it for his own lavish and very conspicuous consumption. By holding grand feasts and hunting expeditions, he proudly displayed his wealth, rank and power to rival chiefs and kings.

Opportunities for hunting
on Islay, 1549

During the reign of Mary Queen of Scots, the Scottish clergyman Donald Monro extolled the pleasures of the Hebrides:

> ...fertil fruitfull and ful of natural graising pasture with mony great deris, mony woods, with fair games of hunting beside every town ...with ane water callit Laxan whereupon mony salmond are slane...[also] the waiter of Griunord which haith sandy banks, upon the quhilk banks upon Eb sea lyis infinite selkis quhilks are slane with doggis lernit to the same effect.

Donald Monro, *Description of the Occidental* [i.e. Western] *Isles of Scotland*, 1549

deris: deer; quhilk: which; upon Eb sea: at ebb-tide; selkis: seals; lernit: trained.

Music and feasting

Some feasts and other entertainments might go on for days. To enjoy a *streah* (round) of drinks, host and guests sat down in a circle; Martin Martin reported that 'it was reckoned a piece of manhood to drink until they got drunk'. Servants stood by with a barrow, to wheel them off to bed. Anyone who left the circle and rejoined it had to apologise to the company in verse, or else pay a fine.

Guests at a feast were carefully seated according to rank and seniority by the chief's stewards. They were entertained by skilled professional performers with music, poems and songs. The *clarsach* (harp) was the most popular instrument, but bagpipes and fiddles were alternatives.

Families of musicians were famous throughout Scotland; it was said that the MacCrimmons, hereditary pipers to the chiefs of Clan MacLeod, learned their music from the fairies. Maybe so, but they also ran a school on Skye to train pipers from many other clans.

BUCHANAN Homeland: Stirlingshire

One day, King James V (d. 1542) went hunting near Kippen, in Clan Buchanan land. As his servants carried fine fat deer back home, clan chief John Buchanan stopped them. 'These belong to the king?' he enquired. 'Then I'll take them – because I am "king" in Kippen!'

These lithographs by R. R. McIan (1803–1856), first published in 1845, show a romanticised, Victorian view of Scottish costume. They must not be regarded as historically accurate.

FARQUHARSON Homeland: *Deeside*

Famous for keeping a Cairn of Memory, near Ballater.
As Farquharson clansmen gathered, ready to go to war, each soldier left
a stone on the cairn. If he returned home safely, he took a stone away
with him. If not, it remained, to record his passing.

GRANT Homeland: Strathspey, northeast Scotland

*Clan Grant and Clan Shaw were enemies; both claimed the same lands.
Around 1580, a Clan Shaw chieftain died fighting; his men buried him
in his ancestral graveyard – which, by then, was in Clan Grant hands.
The Grants dug him up and left his body on his widow's doorstep –
over and over again!*

GUNN Homeland: far north of Scottish mainland

In 1478 Gunn clansmen agreed to hold a Battle of the Champions, to settle a bitter feud with Clan Keith. Twelve top warhorses from each side were allowed to take part. But clan Keith sent two men riding on each charger — and, of course, the Gunns were defeated.

MACDUFF Homeland: Fife and northeast Scotland

*Clan chief's daughter Isabella MacDuff (died c.1314) married the
Count of Buchan. They were not happy. Isabella supported Scots hero
Robert the Bruce, and was captured by Edward I of England. Edward
hung her in a cage – for four years! – outside Berwick castle. This was
not enough for Isabella's husband, who asked Edward to kill her.*

MACINNES Homeland: far west coast

Around 1150, MacInnes clansmen scared away Viking invaders by a clever trick. They marched about dressed first in plaids, then in hairy cattle hides, and then in hides with the smooth side outwards. The Vikings thought the MacInnes army was three times its real size, and prudently retreated.

MACLACHLAN Homeland: Argyll and Loch Fyne

Some clans had peaceful traditions. Chiefs of clan MacLachlan and
their neighbours, the Campbells, went to each other's funerals and lay
on the graves, weeping. This commemorated friendly chiefs who had
fought side by side long ago, and promised to see each other's bodies
safely brought home and buried.

ROSS Homeland: Ross-shire, northern Scotland

Members of Clan Ross were some of the earliest Scots to settle in North America. In 1651 David, 12th Chief of Ross, led 1,000 clansmen to fight against the English Parliament. He was defeated, and many of his followers were deported to English colonies in North America, where they were forced to work like slaves. In 1766 Colonel George Ross (1730-1779) was a signatory of the US Declaration of Independence.

Poet power

Poets were feared as well as admired. Their main task was to praise and celebrate. But unless a chief offered them rich rewards for a performance, they might cruelly mock him in very memorable words, bringing 'great dishonour'. Poets were said to compose their verses by hiding away in a dark room with their plaids over their heads and a heavy stone on their stomachs, ransacking their brains for words and rhymes.

Happy memories?

As the bagpiper was playing, an elderly Gentleman informed us, that in some remote time, the Macdonalds of Glengary having been injured, or offended by the inhabitants of Culloden, and resolving to have justice or vengeance, came to Culloden on a Sunday, where finding their enemies at worship, they shut them up in the church, which they set on fire; and this, said he, is the tune that the piper played while they were burning.

Samuel Johnson, *Journey to the Western Islands of Scotland*, 1775

A piper's duties included waking the chief in the mornings, leading the clan into battle and performing at important occasions such as weddings or funerals. Most hereditary pipers would only play *ceòl-mór* (dignified, serious music, such as praise-songs or laments). Junior pipers played the livelier, jollier *ceòl-beag*, which included tunes for dancing, or to entertain guests at a feast:

That household is not mean or poor
Where the loud sound of the pipes is heard
Followed by the music of harps...

Translation of lines by Mary MacLeod (c.1615–1707), one of the finest Gaelic poets of her age

Hereditary fiddler James MacPherson achieved lasting fame in a rather different way. He is said to have composed 'MacPherson's Rant' as he was being taken to the gallows, to be hanged as an outlaw. His tune is still played today.

A bad start...

Food, just like drink, was served in extravagant quantities. It was shameful for a chief to be thought mean or stingy. In 1540, Ranald 'Galda' ('the stranger' – his mother came from Clan Fraser) was chosen as new leader of Clanranald to replace his brother John, the 8th chieftain, who was languishing in prison. For his inaugural feast, he suggested that a few lowly chickens would be plenty, rather than prime roast beef or deer. His clansmen were horrified. This was not how chiefs should entertain! Ever after, he was known as 'Ranald of the Hens'.

...and a very grand gesture

Other clan chiefs went to the opposite extreme. Few could rival Alasdair Grotach, 8th Chief of Clan MacLeod on the Isle of Skye. Some strange, flat-topped mountains close to the Clan Macleod castle were known as 'MacLeod's Tables'. So, when King James V visited Skye in 1536, Alasdair invited him to a magnificent feast – on top of his very own table mountains.

"

The average clan…
was no more a family than
is a Mafia 'family'.

Arthur Herman, *The Scottish Enlightenment*, 2001, p. 117

"

CHAPTER EIGHT

THE 'HIGHLAND PROBLEM'

'The highlanders and people of the islands…are a savage and untamed nation, rude and independent, given to rapine, ease-loving, clever and quick to learn, comely in person, but unsightly in dress…and exceedingly cruel…'

Around 1370, Scottish Lowland chronicler John of Fordun attempted to write the first comprehensive history of Scotland. As always with historians, his words reveal the opinions of his own era, as well as painting a picture of the past. As we can see, John's view of the clans of the Highlands and Islands was not very favourable. And it was new. Before the 14th century, neither Scottish people nor strangers had spoken of a division between Highlanders and Lowlanders. Everyone was treated as a Scot, all together. What had gone wrong?

From the time of King David I (died 1153), Scottish kings had tried to reduce the power of the clans. Some tried force. In 1249 King Alexander II perished on a failed military expedition to crush clan chiefs in Argyll. In 1263 his son, Alexander III, was more successful, defeating the king of Norway and his allies, Clan MacDonald and Clan MacDougall. But most kings found acting by remote control more effective. They encouraged loyal clans – especially the Campbells and the Gordons, and later the MacKenzies – to police the others for them.

For chiefs of these royal-friendly families, it was a golden opportunity. They could make their own territory more secure and fight against clans that threatened them, all the while demonstrating good behaviour by obeying royal commands. Better still, they got rich (kings often rewarded them by granting them the lands of defeated clans), and, with luck, they might also achieve a noble title and an influential position at the royal court. By around 1450 a large part of Scotland had come under royal control.

To increase their influence still further, powerful clans issued bonds of 'manrent' to the heads of smaller, weaker clans. Scottish kings were far from happy at these arrangements; they thought that manrent encouraged rivalry and conflict between clans. So they outlawed it – three times, in 1457, 1491 and 1555. But still it continued:

Be it kenned [known] to all, me, William Macleod of Dunvegan…I bind and oblige me, my heirs, leally [loyally] and truly, by the faith and truth in my body, to…assist, maintain, and defend, and concur with Lachlan Mackintosh of Dunachton, Captain and Chief of the Clan Chattan, and his heirs, in all and sundrie their actions, causes, quarrels, debates, and invasion of any person or persons whatever, indirectly used or intended contrary to the said Lachlan and his heirs in all time coming…

Bond dated 1588, quoted in *The Celtic Magazine*, 1886

Licence to kill

Kings and their royal councils gave orders to act against hostile, disobedient clans by commissions of fire and sword. These might stop at nothing – not even genocide. In 1528 the earl of Moray was licensed to attack Clan Chattan:

> to their utter destruction, by slaughter, burning, drowning and other means, and leave no creature living of the clan, except for women and bairns.

Quoted in J. L. Roberts, *Feuds, Forays and Rebellions*, Edinburgh UP 1999, p. 36

Any widows and fatherless children were to be transported to Norway or Shetland.

Standing alone

In 1469, thanks to a penalty clause in a marriage agreement, Orkney and Shetland became part of Scotland. The Borders were still a lawless zone, but their reivers did not challenge Scottish kings directly, and were a useful buffer against the English. Now only the MacDonald Lords of the Isles remained independent. They were ambitious to win more land on mainland Scotland; that's why they wanted the earldom of Ross (see page 97). And they were treacherous, as well – at least from the Scottish king's point of view. In 1462 MacDonald clan leaders plotted with Edward IV of England to divide Scotland between them (with a further share going to the exiled leader of Clan Douglas as well).

By 1493 James IV decided he must take action. He sailed with his troops to Dunstaffnage Castle, and brought back, as a captive, the last Lord of the Isles. The chief – a weak man, rejected by his clan, who fought bitterly among themselves to decide who might succeed him – spent the rest of his life under house arrest, mostly in a monastery.

Problems, problems

The king had won! But it was a hollow victory. While the Lords of the Isles were in power, they had kept a kind of peace in their lands. But now there was no strong clan leader to replace them, and the kings in Edinburgh were too far away to take control. And so the next 200 years earned an unenviable nickname – Linn na Creach (the Age of the Forays) – at least in the far west of Scotland, where the Lords of the Isles had once ruled.

The Campbells and their allies seized land in Argyll, but further north, in Lochaber and Kintail, there was big trouble. Personal hatreds and longstanding clan feuds bubbled over. Raids and skirmishes became commonplace, as clans struggled to win land, or hold on to what they had. Even national politics became entangled with clan quarrels. For example, in the Civil War fought between Royalists and Parliamentarians from 1642 to 1651, the Campbells supported Parliament, while most other Lochaber clans backed the king.

Lowlanders such as the 14th-century writer John of Fordun (see page 133) had already remarked on the cultural differences between the Highlanders and the rest of Scotland. The gap grew wider. By around 1600 King James VI of Scotland would be calling Highlanders, and the Islanders, 'utterly barbarous', 'wolves and boars'. To the rest of Scotland, the Highlands had become a 'problem'. They were unbalanced, unstable.

In 1496 King James IV declared that chiefs would be responsible for all crimes committed by their followers. In 1498 he cancelled previous grants of land made to Highland clans; he would give enemy clan land to families he could trust.

This plan, like destroying the Lords of the Isles, had worrying and unforeseen consequences. It broke the bond of loyalty between landowners and the ordinary people living on their lands. If the local laird was no longer their clan chief, why should they obey him?

Once and for all...

James IV's great-grandson, James VI (ruled 1585–1625), was a clever man with plenty of bees in his bonnet. These included pacifying the Highlands and joining them to the Lowlands in one godly, obedient, literate, civilised, Scots-speaking nation (James did not like Gaelic). More than that, James hoped eventually to link the English and Scottish parliaments, and create a united kingdom. He was also short of money, and wanted the (largely imaginary) 'wealth of the Isles'.

At first, like his royal ancestors, James VI tried the law. In 1597 he ordered all Highland clan chiefs to appear before the Privy Council in Edinburgh, with royal charters proving their right to occupy clan lands. James knew that some chiefs had no documents, and that others would not come for fear of being arrested. But the king was adamant: any chief who did not appear would lose his lands.

An awfully big adventure

In 1598 James VI sent a party of Gentlemen Adventurers from Lowland Fife to settle on the Hebridean island of Lewis; the local MacLeod chief had just had his lands confiscated. The Adventurers' task was to impose loyal and Scots-speaking culture on the 'wild' islanders.

They failed; without local help, the stony soil and harsh climate made survival almost impossible. The islanders were in no mood to assist; in fact they attacked repeatedly. In 1609 the Adventurers admitted defeat, sold the land to the ambitious MacKenzie clan, and retreated.

From 1609, King James also sent Scots Protestant clansmen from the Lowlands to settle in what is now Northern Ireland, but that is another story…

Captive chiefs

In 1603 James VI became king of England as well as Scotland; he now had English money, English troops and English warships to help him. It was time for action! He planned a new attack on the clans: this time, to destroy their culture. In 1608 he sent a trusted ambassador to the isle of Mull. The envoy invited nine important chieftains on board his fine ship, to hear a bishop preach and to have dinner – and then sailed away with them. They were prisoners!

The chieftains – three from Clan MacLean, three from Clan MacDonald and one each from Clans MacLeod, MacKinnon and MacQuarrie – were carried off to gaol in the Lowlands, and not released for many months, until they had signed a document that 'bound themselves by the most solemn oaths to future obedience to his Majesty and to the laws of Scotland'.

Those laws included the new Statutes of Iona (1609) – a bitter attack on the traditions of the clans.

The Statutes of Iona

1. New Protestant churches, ministers, services, rules – and an end to Celtic secular marriage (see pages 120–121). (Many clan chiefs and their followers were Roman Catholic, or Episcopalian.)

2. New inns to provide lodgings for travellers, to end 'mere idle wandering' and to stop poor cottagers offering hospitality to people who might be dangerous.

3. All 'vagabonds without visible and honest means of living' to be cleared away. Chiefs' households to be reduced; chiefs' hospitality to be less extravagant.

4. *Sorning* (forced hospitality) and begging to end; no more billeting clan chiefs' soldiers on tenants.

5. To end 'poverty and barbarity', caused by 'extraordinair drinking', the sale of all 'strong wynis and acquavitie' to be banned. Poor people can distil spirits for their own use; clan chiefs can import them.

6. Every man with 60 cows or more (in effect, all clan chiefs and their close relatives) must send his eldest son (or, if no sons, daughter) to school in the Lowlands, until 'they may be found able sufficientlie to speik, reid, and wryte Inglische'. Later, an even stricter condition was added: heirs who could speak no English would not be allowed to inherit. This was probably the most damaging new rule: it divorced future clan chiefs from their families, their language, their clansmen, their traditions, their homelands and their history.

7. Existing rules about carrying guns to be strictly enforced.

8. Chiefs must not give hospitality to wandering bards or other entertainers.

9. Chiefs must be answerable for the good conduct of all their clansmen and women, and must not shelter any wrongdoers or fugitives from justice. They must arrest lawbreakers and hand them over to a judge.

The Statutes of Iona were tough – 'tough and devilish sly', to borrow a phrase from Charles Dickens's *Dombey and Son*.

But James's most savage attack was reserved for one clan only – the MacGregors. For centuries Clan MacGregor had fought against their larger, stronger neighbour, land-hungry Clan Campbell of Glenorchy. Many MacGregors had become 'broken men', without land of their own; they settled on estates belonging to the Campbells, Stewarts, Menzies, Colquhouns and others, but were loyal and obedient only to the chief of their own clan. By the early 1600s they had acquired an unsavoury reputation as thieves and raiders.

After a particularly violent MacGregor attack on the Colquhouns in 1603, King James IV outlawed the whole clan. (The ban would not be repealed until 1755.) MacGregors were encouraged to attack – and kill – their fellow clansmen; a generous reward was offered for the head of a dead MacGregor, together with the chance of a new name and a fresh start away from clan lands.

The most famous MacGregor outlaw was Rob Roy ('Red Robert', 1671–1734). Yes, he had red hair, but it did not cover his whole body, as some lurid stories maintained. A Jacobite in 1689, he later became a successful cattle-drover. From 1711 he waged a bitter feud against the duke of Montrose, was bankrupted, and narrowly escaped transportation. Famous for his generosity to the poor, he also blackmailed wealthy farmers and may have been not only a fraudster but also a spy for the government in London.

Scotland's last outlaw

Ewen MacPhee, born in Glengarry around 1785, became a soldier in the British Army. But he hated army life, killed his commanding officer, and deserted. He eventually sought refuge on an island in Loch Quoich. He built a shelter there, persuaded a 14-year-old Highland lassie to be his wife, and survived by stealing sheep to feed his fast-growing family. MacPhee was finally arrested in 1850 after his wife shot at sheriff's officers investigating reports of sheep-stealing. He died in prison in Fort William.

No more fighting?

The last clan battle in Scotland was fought at Maol Ruadh (say 'Mulroy'), near Fort William, in 1688, between the MacDonells of Keppoch – the most lawless of the clans in a very lawless time and place – and Clan MacIntosh, their long-time enemies. The king had given the MacIntosh chief a charter, granting him the right to occupy the Keppoch lands and making him overlord of the Keppoch MacDonells.

Furiously, the MacDonell chief waved his sword above his head. 'I hold my land by the power of this weapon, not by a scrap of sheepskin!' he said.

But before much longer, even the bravest MacDonell clansman would soon be discovering that sheep were more powerful than swords or parchments. It was the end of an era…

> The traditional clans of old finally perished not on the battlefield so much as in the sheepfold.

Thor Ewing's *Scottish Clans* website,
http://thorewing.net/clans/

CHAPTER NINE

FROM GLENCOE TO BALMORAL

As the crow flies, the distance between two of Scotland's most splendid landscapes, the grim mountains of Glencoe and the sheltered, tree-clad slopes of Balmoral, is not much more than 60 miles (100 km). But they are a world away from each other, in terms of politics as well as atmosphere – and as symbols of Scotland. Glencoe, the site of a shocking clan massacre in 1692, seems full of shadows from the past. Balmoral, home to a fairytale castle completed for Queen Victoria in 1856, looks forward to a modern Scotland of picture postcards and tartan shortbread tins, where clans are a prime asset of the heritage and tourist industries. In this chapter we will look briefly at the years in between the Glencoe massacre and the building of Balmoral, to see how Scotland was changing – fast.

Death in the snow

Clan MacDonald of Glencoe were a small sept (branch) of the once-mighty MacDonald clan. Like their neighbours, the MacDonells of Keppoch, they were notorious cattle raiders. And, like almost all branches of Clan Donald, their leaders were Jacobites.

In 1691 Scottish clan chiefs were ordered to sign an oath of allegiance to King William III by the start of the following year. The chief of Clan MacDonald of Glencoe, Alastair MacIain, missed the deadline (1 January 1692). He had waited for permission from Jacobite leaders overseas, he went to the wrong place to sign (he may have been deliberately misinformed), and he was delayed by atrocious winter weather.

King James for ever!

Jacobites were supporters of King James VII and II (of Scotland and England) and his descendants. In 1689 King James had been exiled by the English and Scottish parliaments. He was replaced on the throne of both countries by his daughter Mary and her Dutch husband, Prince William of Orange. Next, Mary's sister Anne became queen, but when she died in 1714 she left no surviving children. A German prince, George of Hanover, was the nearest Protestant heir, and he became king of the United Kingdom. (There were over 50 royal relatives with a better claim to the throne, but they were all barred because they were Roman Catholics.) There were Jacobites in England and continental Europe, as well as in Scotland.

In 1689, just three years before the massacre at Glencoe, Scottish Jacobites rebelled. 'Bonnie Dundee' led clansmen to win a famous battle (see page 56), but the revolt failed – and it left the London government very, very nervous.

Scottish ministers in the London government decided to make an example of MacDonald. They sent 120 soldiers into Glencoe under the command of a Campbell (traditional enemies of Clan Donald). Following clan tradition, the MacDonald families gave the soldiers food and shelter, for a fortnight. Then, in the dark before dawn on 13 February 1692, the troops turned on their hosts – and attacked them.

The clan chief was shot; his wife was stripped and driven out into the snow, and a soldier gnawed the rings off her chilly fingers. Thirty-six more members of the clan perished from cold or gunfire; 150 survivors were left homeless.

The massacre at Glencoe was far from being the worst atrocity committed in Scotland. Clans themselves had done many more dreadful things to each other. However, government ministers, and King William III, were widely criticised for ordering the killing. They were unrepentant. Clans were the only private armies left in Britain. They were dangerous; a threat to the state. They had to be suppressed.

Culloden, and after

Clansmen joined in several later Jacobite rebellions, notably in 1715, 1719 and 1745. But none of the revolts succeeded. And not all clans were Jacobite: clan chiefs and ordinary clansmen fought in the armies on both sides. The Jacobite cause faded away after 1746, when up to 2,000 clansmen died fighting in the last battle of the final Jacobite rebellion, at Culloden near Inverness.

In the past, it was often said that Culloden marked 'the end of the clans in Scotland'. As we shall see, that is probably not true, although savage reprisals by King George II's government against Jacobite clans after 1746 were designed to crush raiding and fighting in the United Kingdom for ever, and to weaken the ties that bound clans together. They followed on from an act made by King James II himself, in 1682, which had outlawed carrying guns more than 7 miles (11 km) away from home.

Loyal clans

Which clans fought *against* the Jacobites in 1745?

The best-known is Clan Campbell; others included many far-north and northeast clans, such as Gunn, MacKay, Munro, Ross, Sinclair and Sutherland, together with great Lowland families including Clans Cunningham, Kerr and Semphill.

Some clans played no part in the fighting, or were left leaderless after their chiefs were imprisoned. And Jacobite armies included men from the Lowlands and Edinburgh, from Ireland, France and Spain.

In 1746, by Act of Parliament, clan chiefs were stripped once and for all of their powers to catch criminals, to put them on trial or to punish them. The next year, 1747, the wearing of traditional dress was banned throughout the Highlands, together with the carrying, owning or concealment of weapons (including knives), and the playing of bagpipes. Daily prayers for the king were made compulsory in schools.

However, King George II's government did respect the fighting skills of the clansmen who had battled against it. In the 60 years after 1746 over 48,000 Scottish men, mostly Highlanders, were recruited as soldiers in the British Army (where they wore the kilt, and tartan, both of which were prohibited for civilians). They were good, brave soldiers – loyal to their regiments, as well as to those clan chiefs who became army officers. And, as one government minister put it, it was no great loss if they got killed.

A new way of life

Put yourself in the shoes of a Highland clan chieftain some time around 1707, the year Scotland was joined to England to create the United Kingdom (by a vote of the Scottish Parliament, desperate to solve its economic problems). You're not a MacDonell or a MacDonald or a MacGregor, but perhaps a peace-loving chief living in the eastern Highlands, or towards the Lowlands region, or in the Borders. After a century of war (on behalf of your clan, the king, the English Parliament, and rival religious factions), your lands are looking a lot less healthy than they did before. Your family's fields and farms, your woods, your cottages, have been trampled and burned. Your livestock has been driven away, your barns looted.

Your *family's* lands, not your clan's? That's right: by now, you have come to see all these as your personal heritage. And so does Scottish law, and the king.

If you are a good man, with a liking for tradition, you will also consider your clansfolk. You will try to treat them fairly, like the old-style 'father' of a clan. You may even try to help them. But the bond linking you and them has already weakened. The Statutes of Iona (pages 143–144) stopped you from demanding that your clansmen should provide you with food and lodging. And so now they pay you money rent for their fields and cottages. (This puts the burden of transporting and marketing their produce on them.) And – what a change from the past! – clansmen and women now have no security. You can, if you choose, lease them a cottage or land for only one year at a time. You rely on tacksmen to collect rents for you – and they take a share for their trouble, and so you make less money from farming.

You may also spend weeks or months away from the clan homelands, taking part in government business or the law in Edinburgh, hoping to win favour from the king at the royal court in London, or travelling in Italy, or studying in the Netherlands. You may even serve as an officer in the British or French armies, or venture further overseas, to India or the Americas.

Back at home, many of your clansmen and women are very poor. They're lucky to have survived a terrible famine that struck Scotland from 1696 to 1698. After several years of cold summers, grain crops did not ripen, but rotted in the fields. Sheep, goats, cattle, horses died; around one in seven of Scotland's people perished.

You yourself are deeply in debt. You like to live well, following the latest fashions in fine clothes. You buy books, paintings and furniture for your castle or tower-house, and for your town-house in Edinburgh. You enjoy tobacco (smoked in a pipe, or as snuff) from the Caribbean or North America, and brandy or red wine imported from France. You must have horses and weapons (new-style pistols, maybe); you have lawyers' bills to pay. You need to find wages for your servants. In short, you've turned into a landlord, a consumer, an employer. You're not a 'fatherly' chief or a fearsome warlord any more!

To repay your debts, you need money – cash in hand, rather than the traditional tribute handed over by clan followers. Some of your fellow chiefs have taken out *wadsetts* (mortgages); should you do the same? You'll be fine so long as you can pay the interest, but will lose your land if you can't. If you have to borrow, do so from a relative, however distant; that way, if you default on the loan, the land will still stay within the clan.

What are the alternatives? You might consider coal mining, iron furnaces or felling timber; or, like so many other Scottish landowners, stocking your fields with fat black beef cattle to feed fast-growing markets south of the Border. Find a trusty tacksman or a sensible relative to help manage your lands – or hire a businesslike stranger, maybe even from England.

To begin with, you'll want more people on your lands, as well – clan members or non-members. You can lease them smaller and smaller plots of ground. From around 1720, they will plant an exciting new crop: potatoes! And, if your lands are by the sea, they can gather kelp (seaweed, burned to release ash, used in chemical industries) or set up commercial fisheries.

The Highland Clearances

There is another option. By 1750, some of your fellow chiefs have begun to 'clear away' the old, small, unprofitable farms on their estates, to make space for new, intensive, livestock production. Lowland lairds have led the way; now Highland chiefs are following their example. From a commercial point of view, it's sensible to clear 'surplus' tenants off your land, even if they are your fellow clansmen and women. You could encourage them to emigrate to North America, or to settle on little crofts (plots of land too small to live on) on unproductive land. Or they could move to fast-growing towns and cities in Scotland's Central Belt; you'll find that soon there will be nearly as many Gaelic speakers in Glasgow as in the Highlands.

Replace your clansmen with sheep, especially the big, fast-growing, Cheviot breed. Their meat and wool fetch high prices south of the Border – and you'll find that sheep can be four or five times more profitable than people. After all, you know what they say: 'The yield of the ground will depend on the landlord.'

Clearances and crofting

1590s, 1609 Royal laws weaken or abolish traditional links between clan chiefs and people living on their lands.

c.1600–c.1700 Chiefs increase the numbers of cattle kept on their estates; their relatives, and tacksmen, act as cattle drovers, selling cattle at markets in the Lowlands.

1716 Disarming Act bans clan weapons after the 1715 Jacobite rebellion.

1725 General George Wade begins to build new military roads and bridges; these make the Highlands more accessible.

In the same year, clan chiefs' local militias are united to form the Black Watch regiment in the British Army; many landless or hungry clansmen join up.

1730 Start of large-scale sheep farming by clan chiefs and Lowland landlords.

1730s The Duke of Argyll introduces new, commercial, leases on his lands.

1745–1746 Last Jacobite rebellion.

1746 Act of Proscription bans clan weapons, traditional Highland dress, etc. Heritable Jurisdictions Act ends clan chiefs' powers of justice.

1755 Start of large-scale emigration to Canada and North America.

1762 First large-scale sheep farms in the north of Scotland; others soon follow.

1770s Clansmen join British Army in large numbers; British wars overseas increase demand for soldiers.

1784 Confiscated estates are returned to those Jacobite chiefs who have made peace with the government and are no longer thought to be a danger. Many are leased to rich families from the Lowlands or England.

1785 Clan chief MacDonell of Glengarry starts large-scale clearances of his estates. His tenants go to Canada.

1792 'The Year of the Sheep'; rioters attack shepherds and seize sheep in Ross-shire.

1803 Passenger Vessels Act increases the cost of sea travel; landlords try (for a while) to keep tenants on their estates to work as crofters or in kelp and forest industries.

1807–1821 Massive clearances in Sutherland; around 10,000 tenants driven out, with violence. Some settle on small crofts, others emigrate.

1825 Kelp industry collapses; landlords in the Western Islands sell their estates, leaving less work for tenants.

1830s Hunger, cholera, unemployment. Many poor families emigrate.

1845 New Poor Law makes landlords responsible for helping poor tenants; some do this, others remove tenants altogether.

1845–1847 Potato crop fails; famine begins; food riots take place.

1849–1860 Clearances on far west coast, Western Islands and Skye; some families settle on crofts, others emigrate. Many migrants now head for Australia and New Zealand.

1852 Highlands and Islands Emigration Society set up to encourage poor Highlanders to emigrate.

1860 Last of the major clearances, but emigration continues.

1882 Battle of the Braes; crofters on Skye demand rights to occupy land.

1886 Crofters (Holdings) Act; for the first time, crofters have security of tenure.

Romantic Scotland

In 1822 King George IV made a triumphant visit to Edinburgh. By this time the Jacobite threat had long since disappeared, and clansmen no longer lived and worked together under the protection of their chief, on traditional clan lands.

The king was escorted by Scotland's – Britain's – the world's – most famous novelist: Sir Walter Scott (1771–1832). His novels about his country's dramatic, romantic history – featuring clan feuds, clan heroes and clan honour – were wildly popular, along with mock-medieval poems about long-dead clan warriors by 'Ossian' (James MacPherson, 1736–1796). The Edinburgh streets were full of tartan-clad men and women, and the king (clad in tartan) met many splendidly bedecked clan chiefs.

But, in everything real, apart from sentiment and ceremonial, the power of the clans had completely disappeared.

His smooth claymore glittered aloft,
In his champion hand it was light;
And the snoring winds kept moving his locks
Like spray in the whirlpool's might!

The hills on each side they were shaken,
And the path seemed to tremble with fright!
Gleamed his eyes, and his great heart kept
    swelling –
Oh! cheerless the terrible sight!

Description of legendary hero Fingal, from *The Works of Ossian, the son of Fingal* (James MacPherson), 1765

claymore: two-handed broadsword.

It was left to King George IV's niece, Queen Victoria, to rehabilitate the clans. From her first visit, in 1842, she fell in love with Scotland, the 'proudest, finest country in the world'. Victoria loved Scottish scenery, travelled to see clan landmarks, listened to Scottish music, watched Scottish sports and Scottish dancing, surrounded herself with Scottish servants, and covered almost everyone and everything at Balmoral in tartan. She entertained clan chiefs, read Scottish poems and stories about clans, learned about her Scottish royal ancestors (who included many clan leaders), and wrote enthusiastic diaries describing her Scottish holidays.

Yet for Victoria, and for the thousands of her subjects who followed her example and headed north of the Border to enjoy their free time in the latest royal fashion, Scotland was an escape, a refuge, a fantasy shadow of its former self. Their admiration was genuine, but it was for an image rather than reality. The clans, clan chiefs, clansmen and clanswomen who made Scotland, and who featured so largely in its turbulent history, had been shattered and scattered, for ever.

"

History…is what you can remember.

W. C. Sellar and R. J. Yeatman,
1066 and All That, 1930

"

CHAPTER TEN

CLANS TODAY

On 24 July 2009, in Scotland's 'Year of the Homecoming', over 30,000 clansmen, women and children paraded through the streets of Edinburgh. They came from 124 different clans, and from all round the world. What, apart from an evidently most successful marketing drive by VisitScotland, had brought them such a long way to Scotland's capital city? And, less cynically, what made the day such a genuinely joyful occasion? What makes ancient institutions like Scottish clans so popular today? (There are over 2,000 clan societies in the USA alone.) What gives clans purpose and meaning?

Today, clan feuding and fighting are long past. Clan chiefs no longer feed, defend or advise their clansfolk, or play an influential part in politics. Instead, they follow a wide range of careers. Some, like their ancestors, are rich landowners, but other chiefs work as a lorry driver (Clan Gunn), gardener (MacArthur), TV cameraman (MacLeod), accountant (Broun or Brown), optometrist (MacDonell of Keppoch) and Roman Catholic priest (Lamont). Father Lamont is Australian – and, like him, over half the known clan chiefs now live outside Scotland.

Don't know, don't care?

The vast majority of ordinary clan members lead normal, everyday lives far from their ancestral homelands. Unless they are actors, or work in the tourist and heritage industries, they do not routinely drape themselves in tartan and roam across the heather. Many men, women and children of Scottish heritage do not even know – or care – which clan they belong to. This is especially true in Scotland, and is perhaps not quite so peculiar as it might at first appear. Many Jacobite clan members changed their names – typically to something neutral like Black or White – to avoid reprisals after the 1745 rebellion. Later, in the 19th century, thousands of families moved from clan homelands to Scotland's fast-growing industrial cities. There, clans were no longer relevant. Comradeship at work, good-neighbourliness in poor, crowded city slums, and political solidarity when faced by adversity became much more important in the struggle to survive.

Today, some observers claim to detect new 'virtual' clans in Scotland, as old clan ties wither away. These are based on lifestyle choices or communities of interest, such as a liking for Goth music and fashion, or passionate support for a football team.

So, do traditional Scottish clans still have any function today? In 2003 only 32% of Scottish residents sampled by pollsters thought so. Is claiming clan membership anything more than an excuse to put on fancy dress and enjoy a jolly good party at Clan Gatherings at home in Scotland or (much more likely) in Scottish settlements overseas? Opinions are divided…

Kilts and kin

Scots writer John Buchan (1875–1940) claimed that misty-eyed romance was 'a revolt against the despotism of facts'. Many modern clan critics would agree with him. They call the whole 'kilts and kin' image of Scottish clans an invented tradition, or sheer wishful thinking. They claim that looking back to a romantic, idealised Scotland of the clans is an escape, however pleasant, from reality.

A few radicals even criticise today's clan chiefs as relics of a vanished way of life that abused the trust of ordinary people. They accuse chiefs of depriving their followers of their ancestral Scottish homeland. They contrast the profits made from clan-based tourist enterprises owned by a few clan chiefs with the unpaid efforts of countless volunteers belonging to worldwide clan societies who do so much to keep today's clans alive.

Others – Scots or not – describe today's clans as Scotland's unique asset and look forward to a golden age when clans become a truly modern international friendship network.

Scottish and proud of it

For many Scots, at home as well as overseas, that golden age has perhaps already arrived. To them, clans are a living, breathing link between Scotland's past and their own present-day experience:

> It gave me a shock – and a little bit of a thrill – to see ordinary, everyday buses full of shoppers with the fateful word 'Culloden' on their destination boards. I wonder what all those dead clansmen on Culloden battlefield would think of that?
>
> Tourist in Inverness, 2010

Clans give anyone of Scots heritage who wishes to claim it a name, a kin, and a sense of belonging. Perhaps that is why the notion of clan membership is so popular in relatively new nations. 'Home towns' in North America, Australia, New Zealand and other lands settled by Scots may be barely one hundred years old; clan ties may stretch back for one thousand. Good or bad, ancient or modern, true tradition or sheer fantasy, clans provide identity, community, continuity.

Clan myth or history?

* **All clan members are related by blood to each other and to the clan chief.** No. People joined clans in all kinds of ways: they volunteered, they were forced, or they just happened to live on a clan chief's land. Some may have been related to other clan members, some not. Only one in four or five, at the very most, might be distantly related to the clan chief.

* **Each clan has its own unique tartan or tartans.** Only since the 19th century. Before then, anyone could – and did – wear any tartan they chose. Between around 1800 and 1860, romantic enthusiasts for Scottish traditions created the 'system' of clan tartans, aided and abetted by a pair of fraudsters, the Sobieski Stuart brothers. Today, the Scottish Register of Tartans (www.tartanregister.gov.uk) maintains a list of tartans customarily associated with all the different clans, and many others. For more about the history of Tartan, you might like to read the companion volume to this book, *Tartan and Highland Dress: A Very Peculiar History.*

* **Members of clan septs (junior branches) are related to members of their senior clan.** Only if they can show descent from the clan chief's family. There is no official classification of septs or sept names. The lists of septs that appear in books, maps and websites today are based on traditional links between certain family names and certain areas of Scotland; no more, no less.

* **Mc, Mac, M' all mean something different when part of a clan name.** No. They are all just different ways of writing the same Gaelic word, *mac*, meaning 'son'.

* **Clans still own their ancestral homelands.** No. Some clan lands and castles belong to charitable trusts or other public bodies, but most have become the private property of clan chiefs and their families or have been sold to wealthy purchasers. In 2012 it was reported that Russian and Chinese millionaires were planning to join the German, Scandinavian, Arab and other foreign-national 'lairds' who now own almost half of Scotland's ancient clan homelands.

Time to remember

Is ignorance bliss? Is romance more fun? Does misunderstanding clan history matter? Yes, it does – and so does overlooking the sometimes shameful part played by Scottish clans far beyond their homeland.

From around 1600, clan members travelled east to China and the Indian subcontinent. They bought (silks and spices) and sold (opium!). They sailed on Scottish shipping lines and fought in British armies. In Japan, around 1865, Scotsman Thomas Glover founded a company that later became the mighty Mitsubishi Corporation. Just as intriguing, his complicated love-life may have inspired Puccini's opera *Madame Butterfly*.

Other Scots sailed west, to the Americas. From the early 1700s there were Scottish slave owners on sugar plantations, and Scottish tobacco merchants making business deals on both sides of the Atlantic. Many Caribbean people are descended from Scottish fathers and from mothers of African heritage. Today there are more members of the

Campbell clan per square mile in Jamaica than in a square mile of Scotland.

In 1779 there were disgraceful scenes when Robert, the dark-skinned son of slave-owning businessman James Wedderburn, came to Scotland to visit him. James was the son of an executed Jacobite leader. He had gone overseas for safety, made his fortune in Jamaica, and retired to live in a splendid Edinburgh mansion. James gave orders to throw Robert out of the house – and threatened him with gaol if he 'troubled' the Wedderburns any further.

Further north, in the USA, Scotsman William MacKintosh (died 1825), the son of a Scots father and a Native American mother, inherited his mother's high status to become leader of the Creek people. But he agreed to give some ancestral Creek homeland to the government of the USA, and was executed as a traitor. Other Scots made more positive contributions. For example, Hugo Reid (1809–1852) recorded the traditional way of life of Native peoples in California, and campaigned for better treatment of them.

Here and now

Clans are found all round the world, from Arabia to the former USSR. They tell us where we have come from and who we are, and can even hold out lifesaving hopes for the future. For example, in 2003 a pioneering appeal through the Clan Forbes Society of the USA located a bone-marrow donor for the gravely ill granddaughter of the Forbes clan chief in Scotland. Who can say what other new uses might one day be found for old clans?

Clans may be local or transnational; loose-knit and informal or governed by exclusive, archaic, heraldic rules. But everywhere they provide a sense of security and support, especially in troubled times:

> We live in a fast-moving and ever-changing world where our roots and sense of belonging are constantly challenged and under threat....We have an extended and ancient family history and present-day togetherness of which we can be very proud.

Clan chief Madam Arabella Kincaid of Kincaid, 2011

And so, dear reader, let's admire the neat and tidy clan charts and pretty maps and long lists of sept names. Let's smile at the souvenirs, the kilts, the crests, the tartan-covered tourist everything. Let's compete in Highland sports, take part in Highland dances, and even – if we must – play the bagpipes. Let's wear a tartan; whichever one we like. Let's even apply to join a clan! Legally, it's simple: just ask the relevant clan chief to accept you. Let's take a long tour of Scotland's historic clan seats and tragic clan battlegrounds – and enjoy meeting other people who love Scottishtry at Clan Gatherings in our ancient or modern clan homelands. Let's be a clansman or woman or child – and be proud of it!

Because that's the point. Today, as in the past, in spite of their warlike image, clans celebrate and cement friendship and brotherhood. With the world as it right now, the more we have of these pleasant and peaceful feelings, the better!

Appendix

What's my clan?

This partial list of clans and the surnames associated with
them has been compiled from a variety of sources. We
make no claims for it; you may well find conflicting
information in other sources. Note that some names are
associated with more than one clan. Many names have
alternative spellings which are not listed here.

Buchanan Colman, Donleavy, Dove, Dow, Gibb,
Gibson, Gilbertson, Harper, Harperson, Lenny,
Macaldonich, Macandeor, MacAslan, MacCalman,
MacCalmont, MacCammond, MacColman,
MacCruiter, MacDonleavy, MacGibbon,
MacGilbert, MacGreusaich, MacInally, MacIndoe,
MacKinlay, MacMaurice, MacMochie, MacNayer,
MacWattie, MacWhirter, Masterton, Murcheson,
Murchie, Risk, Spittal, Watson, Watt, Yuill.

Cameron Chalmers, Clark, Clarkeson, MacChlerick,
Maclery, MacGillonie, MacIldowie, MacKail,
MacMartin, MacOnie, MacPhail, MacSorlie,
MacVail, Paul, Sorlie, Taylor.

Campbell of Argyll Bannatyne, Burns, Burness,
Denoon, MacDiarmid, MacGibbon, MacGlasrich,
MacIsaac, MacIvor, MacKellar, MacKessock, MacOran,
MacOwen, MacTavish, MacThomas, MacUre,
Tawesson, Thomas, Thomason, Thompson, Ure.

Campbell of Cawdor Caddell, Calder, Cawdor.

Colquhoun Cowan, Kilpatrick, Kirkpatrick, MacCowan.

Davidson Davie, Davis, Dawson, Kay, Keay, MacAye, MacDade, MacDavid.

Farquharson Coutts, Farquhar, Findlay, Finlayson, Greasach, Hardie, Lyon, MacCaig, MacCardnay, MacEarachar, MacFarquhar, MacHardie, MacKerchar, MacKinlay, Reoch, Riach.

Fergusson Fergus, Ferries, MacAdie, MacFergus, MacKerras, MacKersay.

Forbes Bannerman, Fordyce, Michie.

Fraser Frisell, MacGruer, MacKim, MacKimmey, MacShimis, MacSimon, Sim, Simpson, Syme, Tweedie.

Gordon Adam, Adie, Edie, Huntly.

Graham Allardice, Bontine, MacGibbon, MacGilvernoch, MacGreive, Menteith, Monteith.

Grant Gilroy, MacGilroy, MacIlroy.

Gunn Gallie, Gaunson, Georgeson, Henderson, Jamieson, Johnson, Keans, Keene, MacComas, MacCorkill, MacIan, MacKames, MacKean, MacOmish, MacRob, MacWilliam, Manson, Nelson, Robison, Sandison, Swanson, Williamson, Wilson of Caithness.

Lamont Lamb, Lammie, Lamondson, Landers, Lucas, Luke, MacClymont, MacGillegowie, MacIlduie, MacLucas, MacLymont, Meikleham, Turner, Whyte.

Leslie Abernethy, More.

MacArthur Arthur, MacCarter.

MacAulay of Dumbartonshire MacPheidran.

MacBain Bean, MacBeth, MacIlvain, MacVean.

MacDonald Connell, Darroch, Donald, Donaldson, Drain, Galbraith, Gilbride, Gorrie, Gowan, Gowrie,

Hawthorn, Henderson, Johnstone, Kean, Kellie,
Kinnell, MacBeth, MacBride, MacCaish, MacCall,
MacCash, MacCeallach, MacCodrum, MacColl,
MacConnell, MacCook, MacCuish, MacCuithean,
MacDrain, MacEachen, MacEachran, MacElfrish,
MacElheran, MacGorrie, MacGowan, MacGown,
MacHenry, MacHugh, MacHutcheon, MacIan,
MacIlreach, MacIlrevie, MacIlvride, MacIlwraith,
MacKean, MacKellachie, MacKellaig, MacKelloch,
MacKinnell, MacLaivish, MacLardy, MacLarty,
MacLaverty, MacMurchie, MacMurdo, Mac
O'Shanning, MacQuistin, MacRaith, MacRory,
MacShannachan, MacSporran, MacSwan,
MacWhannell, Martin, Reoch, Rorison.

MacDonald of Clanranald MacEachan, MacGeachie,
MacGeachin, MacIsaac, MacKeachan, MacKechnie,
MacKichan, MacKissock, MacVarish.

MacDonald of Keppoch MacGillivantie, MacGilp,
MacGlasrich, MacKillop, MacPhilip, Ronald, Ronaldson.

MacDougall Connacher, Cowan, Dougall, Dowall,
MacConnachie, MacCowl, MacCulloch, MacDowall,
MacKichan, MacLucas, MacLugush, MacLullich.

MacDuff Duff, Fife, Fyfe, Spence, Spens, Wemyss.

MacFarlane Allan, Bartholomew, Caw, Galbraith,
Greisich, Kinnieson, MacAllan, MacAndrew,
MacCause, MacCaw, MacCondy, MacEoin, MacGaw,
MacGeoch, MacJames, MacJock, MacNair,
MacNidder, MacNitter, MacRob, MacWalter,
MacWilliam, Monach, Parlane, Stalker, Weir.

MacGillivray Gilroy, MacGilroy, MacGilvra,
MacIlroy, MacIlvrae.

MacGregor Black, Comrie, Fletcher, Gregor, Gregory, Grier, Grierson, Grig, King, Leckie, MacAdam, MacAra, MacAree, MacChoiter, MacGrowther, MacGruther, MacIlduy, MacLeister, MacLiver, MacNie, MacPeter, Malloch, Peter, Whyte.

MacInnes Angus, Innes, MacAinsh, MacAngus, MacCanish, MacMaster, MacNish, Naish.

MacIntyre MacTear, Tyre, Wright.

MacKay Bain, Bayne, MacCay, MacCrie, MacGee, MacKee, MacPhail, Macquey, MacQuoid, MacVail, Neilson, Paul, Polson, Robson, Williamson.

MacKenzie Kenneth, Kennethson, MacBeolan, MacConnach, MacMurchie, MacVanish, MacVinish, Murchie, Murchison.

MacKinnon Love, MacKinnon, MacKinny, MacMorran, MacNiven.

Mackintosh Clark, Combie, Crerar, Dallas, Elder, Esson, Glen, Glennie, Hardie, MacCardnie, MacChlerich, MacCombie, MacFell, MacGlashan, MacHardy, MacKeggie, Macomie, MacPhail, MacRitchie, MacThomas, Noble, Ritchie, Shaw, Tarrill, Tosh, Toshack.

MacLachlan Ewan, Ewing, Gilchrist, Lachlan, MacEwen, MacGilchrist.

MacLean Beath, Beaton, Black, MacBeath, MacCormich, MacFadyen, MacIlduy, MacLergan, MacRankin, MacVeagh, Rankine.

MacLennan Lobban, Logan.

MacLeod, Sìol Thorcuill Callum, MacAskill, MacAulay of Lewis, MacNicol, Malcolm, Nicol, Nicolson, Tolmie.

MacLeod, Sìol Thormaid Beaton, Bethune, MacCrimmon, MacLure, MacRaild.

Macmillan Baxter, Bell, Brown, MacBaxter.

Macnab Abbot, Dewar, Gilfillan, MacIndeor.

MacNaughton Henry, Kendrick, MacBrayne, MacHenry, MacKendrick, MacNight, MacVicar.

MacNeill MacNeilage, MacNelly, Neill.

MacPherson Catanach, Clark, Currie, Fersen, Gillespie, Gillies, Gow, Less, MacChlerich, MacChlery, MacCurrach, MacGowan, MacLeirie, MacLeish, MacMhuirich, MacMurdo, Murdoch.

MacPhie Duffy, MacGuffie, MacHaffie.

MacQuarrie MacCorrie, MacGorrie, MacGuaran, MacGuire, MacQuhirr, MacWhirr, Wharrie.

MacRae MacAra, MacCraw, MacRa, Macrach, MacRaith, Rae.

MacWilliam Baxter, Bell, Brown.

Matheson MacMath, MacPhun, Mathie.

Menzies Dewar, MacIndow, MacMinn, MacMones, Means, Mein, Mennie, Meyners, Monzie.

Munro Dingwall, Foulis, MacCulloch, MacLullich, Vass, Wass.

Murray Fleming, MacMurray, Moray, Rattray, Small, Spalding.

Ogilvie Airlie, Gilchrist, MacGilchrist.

Robertson Donachie, Duncan, Dunnachie, Inshes, MacConnachie, MacDonachie, MacInroy, MacLaggan, MacRobie, Reid, Roy, Skene, Stark.

Ross Anderson, Andrew, Gillanders, MacAndrew, MacTaggart.

Sinclair Caird, Clyne.

Stewart Boyd, Garrow, Lennox.
Stewart of Appin Carmichael, Combich, Livingstone, MacCombech, MacLeay, MacMichael.
Stewart of Atholl Gregor, Macglashan.
Stewart of Galloway Carmichael, MacMichael.
Stewart of Garth Cruickshanks, Duilach.
Stuart of Bute Bannatyne, Fullarton, Jameson, MacCamie, MacCaw, MacCloy, MacKirdy, MacLewis, MacMutrie.

Clans online

The following websites carry useful information about clans and septs:

http://www.clans-families.org/clan-septs.html
http://www.electricscotland.com/webclans/septs.htm
http://www.electricscotland.com/webclans/alphabetical.htm

Sites concerned with clan tartans are also worth a look:
http://www.tartansauthority.com/tartan-ferret
http://www.tartanregister.gov.uk/search.aspx

In addition, many individual clan societies have websites of their own, which you can find by typing your clan name or surname into any Internet search engine.

Glossary

Alba (Gaelic) Scotland.

Auld Lang Syne (Scots) 'Times Long Ago': a poem written or adapted by Robert Burns, traditionally sung at Hogmanay (New Year) and other occasions.

baile (Gaelic) A village or cluster of cottages.

bannock (Scots) A flat cake of oatmeal or barley.

boll An old Scottish measure of dry weight; about 140 lb (63.5 kg).

broken clan A clan without land.

broken man A person without clan membership and/or clan homeland.

Celtic Belonging to the Celts, a people who lived in Europe from around 800 BC to AD 400, who spoke related languages and shared many cultural practices.

ceòl beag (Gaelic) 'Small music': cheerful, lively songs and tunes.

ceòl mór (Gaelic) 'Great music': solemn tunes and laments.

cineal (Gaelic) Kindred.

clan (from Gaelic) Children, family. Now refers to a large, far-flung group of people all acknowledging the same clan chief and, usually, having the same surname.

clarsach (Gaelic) Harp.

claymore (from the Gaelic) A long sword, carried by clan chiefs and given by them to clansmen.

crofter A tenant of a croft: a small plot of farmland often with poor or unproductive soil.

dùthchas (Gaelic) Ancestral homeland; place of belonging.

Episcopalian A member of a Protestant church that continued many Catholic traditions, especially Church guidance and government by bishops.

fiery cross Two partly burned sticks tied together, sometimes smeared with blood, carried by speedy messengers to summon clansmen to battle.

Gaelic A Celtic language, still spoken in Scotland and Ireland, closely related to Welsh, Cornish and Breton.

gallowglass (from Gaelic) A Scottish mercenary soldier; most fought overseas, especially in Ireland

girnal or **girnal house** (Scots) A barn for grain.

inbye (Scots) Better-quality farmland close to a township.

Jacobite A supporter of King James VII and II (deposed 1689 as King of England, Scotland and Ireland) and his descendants who later claimed to be rightful rulers of Britain.

kinship Membership of a group linked by ties of blood.

Lochaber axe A twin-bladed axe on a long pole, named after the district around Fort William.

mormaer (from Gaelic) A king's deputy; a junior king.

munro Any mountain in Scotland over 3,000 ft (914.4 m). To 'bag' a munro is to climb to its summit.

outbye (Scots) Poor-quality farmland, mostly used for grazing, on the outskirts of a township.

Parliamentarian A supporter of the English Parliament during the Civil War (1642–1651). Some Scottish clans supported Parliament; others, led by the Great Montrose, supported the King.

Scottish Clans

reiver (Scots) A clan or clansman who feuded and raided in the Borders region of Scotland.

Royalist A supporter of King Charles I during the Civil War.

runrig (Scots) A system of sharing small portions of inbye and outbye farmland in townships.

saga A long, epic story in verse or prose, recording the history of people or places. Originally told in Iceland.

seanchaidhean (Gaelic) A clan historian and/or bard.

sept A junior branch of a clan.

sheiling (from Gaelic) A small hut or shelter in upland pastures, where women and young people led cattle to graze during the summer months.

sib (Scots) A brother or sister.

siol (Gaelic) Seed, progeny.

sliochd (Gaelic) Descendants.

sorning (Scots) The traditional custom of demanding hospitality from clan families for the clan chief's troops or servants.

tacksman (Scots) A senior tenant, holding farmland or farm buildings directly from a clan chief. He might sublet small portions of the land, and/or small cottages, to poorer families, known as 'cottars'.

tanaiste (Gaelic) The nominated heir of a king or chief.

taoiseach (Gaelic) Leader or chief.

targe A small round shield.

tocher (Scots) The dowry or portion brought by a bride to her husband's family.

township The same as *baile*, above.

tribute Taxes paid in goods.

wadsett (Scots) A mortgage.

Index

Cherished ⊕ Library

Some other
Very Peculiar Histories™

Scotland
Fiona Macdonald

Vol. 1: From Ancient Times to Robert the Bruce
ISBN: 978-1-906370-91-6

Vol. 2: From the Stewarts to Modern Scotland
ISBN: 978-1-906714-79-6

Robert Burns
Fiona Macdonald
ISBN: 978-1-908177-71-1

Scottish Tartan and Highland Dress
Fiona Macdonald
ISBN: 978-1-908759-89-4

Castles
Jacqueline Morley
ISBN: 978-1-907184-48-2

Scottish Words
Fiona Macdonald
ISBN: 978-1-908759-63-4

Golf
David Arscott
ISBN: 978-1-907184-75-8

Whisky
Fiona Macdonald
ISBN: 978-1-907184-76-5

For the full list, visit
www.book-house.co.uk/History/Cherished

Or go to **shop.salariya.com** to buy direct,
with **free** postage and packaging